Real Estate Tax Handbook
2020 Edition

By

Michael Gray, CPA with Thi T. Nguyen, CPA

Copyright Notices

© 2008, 2014, 2018, 2020 Michael Gray, CPA

ALL RIGHTS RESERVED.

No part of this book may be reproduced or transmitted for resale or use by any party other than the individual purchaser who is the sole authorized user of this information. Purchaser is authorized to use any of the information in this publication for his or her own use only. All other reproduction or transmission, in any form or by any means, electronic or mechanical, including photocopying, recording or by any informational storage or retrieval system, is

prohibited without express written permission from the publisher.

LEGAL NOTICES:

While all attempts have been made to provide effective, verifiable information in this book, neither the author nor publisher assumes any responsibility for errors, inaccuracies, or omissions. Any slights of people or organizations are unintentional.

If advice concerning tax, legal, compliance, or related matters is needed, the services of a qualified professional should be sought. This publication is designed to provide accurate and authoritative information in regard to the subject matter covered. It is sold with the understanding that the publisher is not engaged in rendering legal, accounting, or other professional service. If legal advice or other expert assistance is required, the services of a competent professional person should be sought.

Due to the nature of real estate and varying rules regulating business activities in many fields, some practices proposed in this book may be deemed unlawful in certain circumstances and locations. Since federal and local laws differ widely, as do codes of conduct for members of professional organizations and agencies, the licensee must accept full responsibility for determining the legality and/or ethical character of any and all business transactions and/or practices adopted and enacted in his or her particular field and geographic location, whether or not those transactions and/or practices are suggested, either directly or indirectly, in this book.

As with any business advice, the reader is strongly encouraged to seek professional counsel before taking action. NOTE: No guarantees of savings or profits are intended by this book. Many variables affect each individual's results. Your results will vary from the examples given.

Michael Gray, CPA has no control over what you may do or not do with this book, and therefore cannot accept the responsibility for your results. You are the only one who can initiate action in order to reap your own rewards!

Published by:
Silicon Valley Publishing Co.
2482 Wooding Ct.
San Jose, CA 95128-4271
United States of America

ISBN 978-1-7324865-2-2

For more information

Are you seeking a speaker for your group about real estate tax issues? Are you seeking a resource for a story about real estate tax issues?

Thi T. Nguyen, CPA is available for a limited number of presentations about real estate tax issues and for media interviews. For more information, call (408)286-7400, extension 206 or write Thi T. Nguyen, CPA, Koehler & Associates CPAs, Inc., 1541 The Alameda, San Jose, CA 95126 or email thi@koehlercpa.com.

Michael Gray, CPA has a monthly email newsletter, Michael Gray, CPA's Tax and Business Insight. You can subscribe at no charge or obligation at www.taxtrimmers.com. His general tax website is www.taxtrimmers.com, his real estate tax website is www.realestateinvestingtax.com and his tax isssues blog is www.michaelgraycpa.com.

Praise for
The Real Estate Tax Handbook

"Finally a tax book written just for real estate investors! Michael has done a magnificent job of simplifying a complicated subject so even a beginner can understand the tax consequences of real estate deals before they have to pay huge penalties due to ignorance. It's a must read."

Ron LeGrand
"The Millionaire Maker"
Real Estate Investing Teacher
Global Publishing, Inc.
Jacksonville, Florida

"Mike distills the essence of what a reader needs to know when asking a "what if" question concerning real estate and federal tax implications. The explanations are filled with detailed examples that help enlighten the reader and make the consequences of a given event clear.

"This handbook makes an excellent addition to any real estate broker, agent, investor or accountant's arsenal of tools to use in the trade."

Thomas E. Kaljian, Real Estate Broker
T. Kaljian Real Estate
Los Banos, California

"Mike has taken the complex Internal Revenue Code and given us an excellent resource to understand real estate taxation."

Ed Graziani
Real Estate Agent
Sereno Group
Los Gatos, California
Real Estate Investor
Beldomfia Properties, LLC
Los Altos, California

"You have covered a wide variety of the most important real estate tax issues in a timely, intelligent and efficient manner. While such a publication is never a substitute for the help of a professional tax adviser, this material will educate any individual seeking to achieve important tax objectives related to real estate, and will help make such a consultation more valuable and cost-effective."

G. Scott Haislett, Attorney at Law
Lafayette, California

"I enjoyed very much our discussion today about your upcoming publication of the Real Estate Tax Handbook. This is an outstanding service to homeowners and real estate investors. You are providing the real estate investing public with a useful tool for understanding and working with complicated tax issues and techniques. The Real Estate Tax Handbook is a positive, proactive piece of work that is readable and practical in its approach to real estate investing and its tax pitfalls and opportunities. You clearly know how to communicate on the client level in an action-oriented manner. This is a 'must read' for both real estate investors and tax practitioners as well. Best wishes for success with the book."

Owen G. Fiore, Wealth Planning Consultant
Fiore Wealth Planning Consulting
Kooskia, Idaho

"Michael Gray's Real Estate Tax Handbook is a terrific resource for anyone owning real property, whether it is a basic home, investment property, or commercial development property. It covers a wide range of income tax issues facing property owners, and gives them enough detail to point them in the right direction. It is a great starting point for anyone with income tax questions about the real property they own."

William D. Mahan
Attorney at Law, LLM Taxation
Campbell, California

"A family's real estate investments usually constitute the largest financial investment within their lifetime… In the Real Estate Tax Handbook, 2008 Edition, Michael Gray lets the reader access some of his 30 years experience as a CPA and tax advisor to gain an overview of the financial aspects of real estate.

"For most homeowners, the information contained in the first 30 pages will show them the most important tax implications of buying and selling principal residences, timeshares, and the like, and Chapter 9 outlines mortgage interest deductions.

"Also included are timely issues such as short sales, foreclosures, deeds in lieu of foreclosure, inheritances, trusts, S corporations, 1031 exchanges and issues regarding commercial properties and their impact on taxes.

"This is accomplished in a conversational style, though, of necessity, the mathematics of the topics must be advanced in practical examples. Fortunately, through the table of contents, the reader can review the information that is pertinent to their situation. . . .

"With the complexity of current tax codes, it becomes clear that, with any real estate transaction, a . . . financial professional who is intimately acquainted with tax implications should be consulted."

Steve Gray, Realtor (30 years)
Village Square Realty
Los Gatos, California

Table of Contents

Copyright Notices 4

For more information 5

Praise for the Real Estate Tax Handbook 6

i Introduction 14

1 Sale of a Principal Residence 16
    Goodbye to these familiar old rules! 16
    Some winners, some losers 16
    The exclusion amounts 16
    Frequency of sales limit – ownership and use tests 17
    Reduction of "second residence" exclusion/Reduction of exclusion for "nonqualified use" after 2008 17
    Ownership and use of prior residences 20
    Incapacitated taxpayers 20
    Divorced taxpayers 20
    Widowed taxpayers 20
    Married individuals 20
    Other joint owners 21
    Gain recognized for depreciation 21
    Exclusion prorated 21
    Homeowners in military service, foreign service and federal intelligence 21
    Certain expatriates 22
    Involuntary conversions 22
    Losses are generally not deductible 22
    Repossession by seller 22
    Federal tax rates on long-term capital gains for individuals 22
    Observations 23
    Transferring a family residence to family members at a discount – with two "catches"! 24

2 Other Sales of Real Estate 26
    Qualifying for favored tax rates 26
    Capital gains and losses 26
    Sales of real estate used in a trade or business or for rental 27
    Section 1245 gain (ordinary income) 28
    Section 1250 property (most depreciable real estate) 29
    Other special types of real estate 30
    Section 1231 gains and losses (gains and losses for business property not taxed as depreciation recapture.) 30
    Sale of depreciable property to a related person 31
    Selling expenses 31

Earnest money deposits 31
Option to purchase 32
How to avoid paying tax for personal or investment real estate sales with a "catch" –
Charitable Remainder Trusts 32

3 Foreclosures, Deeds in Lieu of Foreclosure and Short Sales 35
How are foreclosures (and deeds in lieu of foreclosure) taxed? 35
Tax relief enacted for recourse mortgage on principal residence debt forgiveness
(expires after 2021). 37
Disqualified debt taxable first 39
California debt cancellation tax relief for homeowners (expired December 31, 2013) 40
What happens with a "short sale"? 40
What about selling expenses for a recourse mortgage? 41
Other exceptions for cancellation of debt income 42
What if the fair market value of the home has dropped after purchase? 42
Considerations for rental real estate 43
California liability relief for Short Sales 44
California extends nonrecourse protection when refinancing certain mortgages 44

4 Installment Sales 46
What is an installment sale? 46
Planning benefits of installment sales 46
Certain items treated as cash received in the year of sale 46
What property isn't eligible for installment sale reporting? 46
How is the election made? 47
Why elect to not use the installment method? 47
Ordinary income from depreciation recapture isn't eligible for installment sale reporting 47
Income subject to highest rate is taxed first 47
How the taxable gain is computed each year 48
Wrap around mortgages 48
Example with and without a wrap around mortgage 49
Like-kind exchanges 51
Sale of principal residence 52
Mixed property sales 52
Insufficient or unstated interest for installment sale note 53
Interest charge due to IRS for some installment sales 53
Repossessions 55
Sales to related persons who resell the property 56
Sale of depreciable property to a related person 57
Borrowing with installment sale note used as security 57
Contingent payment sales 58
Interest charge for sales by dealers of timeshares and residential lots 58
Suspended passive activity losses and installment sales 59
A corporate tax trap – the alternative minimum tax (repealed) 59
Income with respect of a decedent 60

"Cutting Edge" estate planning strategy – installment sale to a "defective" grantor trust 62
Conclusion 63

5 Tax-Deferred Section 1031 Real Estate Exchanges 64
What can be exchanged? 64
Tenants in common interests or "TICs" 66
Alternative trust arrangements 66
Is an election required? 67
What about losses? 67
When must a gain be recognized? 67
Special rule for Section 1250 property 68
Allocating basis for acquired properties 69
Non-simultaneous exchanges 69
Reverse exchanges 72
Sale of a principal residence acquired as part of a tax-deferred exchange 72
Installment sale reporting for like-kind exchanges 73
Cost segregation and like-kind exchanges 73
Related party exchanges 74
Like-kind exchanges of foreign and U.S. property 74
Vacation rental homes 75
Reporting like-kind exchanges 75
Conclusion - Get Help! 76

6 What are the different forms available for real estate operations? ... 77
Sole ownership 78
Joint tenancy 78
Tenants in common or undivided interests 79
Community property 79
Estate planning trusts 81
"Title" trusts 83
General partnerships 84
Limited partnerships 85
Limited Liability Companies (LLCs) 86
The Centralized Partnership Audit Regime 88
Regular, or C Corporations 89
S Corporations 91
Real Estate Investment Trusts (REITs) 94

7 Depreciation and Cost Segregation 96
Modified Accelerated Cost Recovery System (MACRS) 98
Section 179 Expense election 98
Bonus depreciation 100
De minimis expensing 100
Land v. improvements 101
Demolition of structure 101

Depreciation rules for different classes of assets. ...101
Qualified improvement property. ...103
Foreign-use property ...104
Alternative minimum tax ...104
Cost segregation studies. ...104
Tax-deferred exchanges and involuntary conversions. ...106
Depreciation of the depreciable exchanged basis. ...106
Depreciation of the depreciable excess basis. ...107
Property surrendered wasn't depreciated using MACRS. ...107
Election to not apply rules for replacement property. ...107
Facilitative costs. ...107

8 At Risk Limitation, Passive Activity Loss Limitation and Excess Business Loss Limitation ...110

At Risk Limitation. ...110
Passive Activity Loss Limitations ...111
What are separate activities? ...112
Rental real estate activities. ...112
Real estate professionals. ...114
Election to treat all rental properties as one activity. ...115
Rental of nondepreciable property. ...115
Net income from rental to related entity. ...116
Self-charged interest. ...116
Rental of residence. ...116
Material participation. ...116
Limited partners. ...117
Limited liability company members. ...117
Publicly-traded partnerships. ...118
Passive assets and estate tax deferral. ...118
Excess business losses of noncorporate taxpayers. ...119

9 Deducting Mortgage Interest ...121

Types of interest. ...121
What is a qualified indebtedness for the acquisition or improvement of a residence? ...122
What happens when you refinance a mortgage secured by a qualified residence? ...124
Refinancing rental properties ...124
Refinancing through passthrough entities. ...124
Points ...125
Limitation on deduction for business interest ...126

10 Repairs – Current Deduction or Capitalized? ...128

New safe harbor for "small taxpayers". ...128
Safe harbor for routine maintenance ...130
Building systems. ...131
Leased buildings. ...132

Michael Gray | 11

Repairs done before a building is placed in service 132
Repairs incidental to improvements 132
Removal costs 132
Repairs to residence incidental to improvements (remodeling) 133
Personal and other real property 133
Improvements that must be capitalized 133
Election to capitalize repair and maintenance costs 135
Partial dispositions 135

11 Family Limited Partnerships (FLPs) - How to Reduce Your Estate Tax For A Family Business Or Real Estate Investments By 35% Or More! 137
The benefits of lifetime giving 138
Caution! 138
Family wealth planning using a family partnership or LLC holding real estate 138
Using entity fractionalization for investment assets 139
What the IRS doesn't want you to know 140
Properly implementing a family wealth plan is a worthwhile investment 140
When does entity fractionalization make sense? 140

12 Holding Real Estate in an IRA, Roth or Retirement Account 141
Roth accounts – special benefit power 141
Who will be the trustee/administrator of the plan? 142
Unrelated business income 142
Unrelated debt-financed income 144
Prohibited transactions 144
Valuation concerns 145

13 Materials and Supplies 147
Materials and supplies 147
Standby emergency spare parts 148
Rotable and spare parts 148
De Minimis with an applicable financial statement 148
De Minimis rule with no applicable financial statement 149
Some items must still be capitalized 150

14 Net Investment Income Tax 151
Legal challenge to the Net Investment Income Tax 151
How do you compute the NII tax? 152
What is net investment income? 153
Passive activities, real estate professionals and the NII tax 153
Gains and losses 154
Tax planning strategies for the NII tax 154
Get professional help 155

15 The Deduction For Noncorporate Business Income (Passthrough Deduction) 156
Which taxpayers are eligible 157
A new deduction category...157
How do you compute the deduction?..157
Does rental real estate income qualify?...158
Safe harbor for rental real estate. 158
What if you don't elect the safe harbor? 160
Does claiming rental real estate as a trade or business give you a tax benefit? 160
Specified service businesses..160
The business of being an employee..161
Aggregation of businesses 161
Which wages are used for the limitation?...162

16 Qualified Opportunity Zones – A New Opportunity To Defer or Avoid Federal Income Tax on Capital Gains 163
A summary of tax benefits...163
How the election is made...164
What is reinvested? 164
What will be the character of the gain when it's taxable?..................164
Be prepared..164
How is the investment done?..165
Eligible gain..165
The 180-day replacement period beginning date 165
Eligible gains realized by a partnership 167
Inclusion events...167
Covid-19 deadline extensions..168

Michael Gray | 13

i
Introduction

As I update this book during 2020, the tax development for real estate since the book was last updated in 2018 have mostly been evolutionary, with the exception of a technical correction making certain improvements to real estate eligible for bonus depreciation in the CARES Act of 2020. Besides that, we have mostly been getting guidance from the IRS relating to changes in the Tax Cuts and Jobs Act of 2017.

Remember many of the changes enacted in the Tax Cuts and Jobs Act of 2017 are scheduled to expire after 2025. I am writing these updates before the Presidential election during November 2020. If Joe Biden is elected President of the United States and the Democrats win control of the Senate, there will probably be more significant tax legislation during 2021.

The real estate markets have made an uneven recovery after the collapse of 2008. In my home area of Silicon Valley, there is a boom in residential real estate prices, mostly due to scarce inventory. Very few homeowners are offering their homes for sale.

Regardless of the economic climate, real estate plays an important role in our lives. We have to sleep, eat, work, play, learn and worship somewhere. A modification may be telecommuting in cyberspace, but we even have to park our computer and find a seat somewhere when we work for an extended period of time. Somewhere means real estate will be involved.

When you consider the many functions of real estate and how it's intertwined with so many aspects of our lives, you can appreciate why there are so many tax considerations that apply to real estate.

In the process of a career as a tax consultant for more than forty years, helping clients with real estate transactions has been a key area of my practice.

Rather that write an in-depth tax treatise for tax practitioners, I decided to write about highlights of real estate problems and opportunities for homeowners and real estate investors, with a recommendation to consult with a professional tax consultant relating to how the rules apply to your particular facts.

In this book, homeowners and investors will find practical, focused, and positive ideas for action.

I intentionally haven't extensively documented the text. The footnote references are for convenience when questions come up.

Also remember to check for state tax consequences of your transactions. Many states have tax rules that don't conform to the Internal Revenue Code. For example, California taxes long-term capital gains at the same tax rates as ordinary income.

Tax advisors might find this book to be useful as a checklist of real estate tax compliance and planning issues.

I can't cover everything relating to U.S. income taxation of real estate in this book, but tell me about any major omissions or corrections that you discover at mgray@taxtrimmers.com, and I'll include them in later editions of this book.

Whenever we write about tax laws, we have a moving target. Tax laws change regularly, including new rulings by the courts and the IRS, new Treasury Regulations, and new tax laws passed by Congress. Investors should consult with tax advisors about these matters. Tax advisors must be alert for developments and perform research to support their advice.

Effective January 1, 2018, I sold my tax consulting and tax return preparation practice to Ms. Thi T. Nguyen of Koehler & Associates CPAs, Inc. She is collaborating with me for this update of the Real Estate Tax Handbook.

If you have additional questions relating to real estate tax issues, you can contact Thi at her email address, thi@koehlercpa.com.

Enjoy!

Michael Gray, CPA
September 3, 2020

1
Sale of a Principal Residence

Thanks to legislation enacted during 1997 and subsequent guidance issued by the IRS and later modifications by Congress, the rules of the game have been dramatically changed relating to the sale of a principal residence. There are significant tax planning opportunities in the new rules, but some taxpayers will be worse off. Many of the old concepts have been repealed, so we need to adapt our thinking to the new rules.

You might think it's strange that I'm referring to the pre-1997 rules for sale of a residence in a current explanation, but I still get questions from people who are confused because they remember the old rules or a friend is giving advice based on them.

Goodbye to these familiar old rules!

For example, previously we were concerned with replacing the residence with another residence with a purchase price equal to or exceeding the selling price of the former residence within a certain time frame. That rule has been repealed. No replacement residence is required. Each residence stands on its own.

Previously, "fixing up expenses" were a factor in determining the deferred gain with respect to a principal residence. Fixing up expenses are no longer part of the computation under the new rules.

Previously, taxpayers age 55 or over were eligible to exclude $125,000 of gain from the sale of a principal residence. Under the new rules, taxpayers age 55 or over are treated the same as other taxpayers.

Some winners, some losers

Sometimes there are winners and losers of tax changes. There will be some losers in Silicon Valley under this provision. Members of Congress couldn't envision middle class homes appreciating more than $500,000, as some have in Silicon Valley and other areas.

The exclusion amounts

Under the current rules, an individual may exclude from income up to $250,000 ($500,000 on a joint return) of gain realized from the sale of a principal residence. Notice this limit isn't adjusted for inflation. $500,000 is worth a lot less now than when the limitation was adopted in 1997.

Taxpayers may elect to recognize the gain from the sale of their residence. A taxpayer could decide to do this if the gain was small and the election enabled the taxpayer to claim the exclusion for another residence within the two-year period with a bigger gain.

Frequency of sales limit – ownership and use tests

The exclusion applies to one sale or exchange every two years. Sales before May 7, 1997 are not taken into account. The home is not required to be the principal residence at the time of purchase or sale; it only needs to meet the ownership and use tests.

Under the ownership test, the individual must have owned the residence as a principal residence for a total of at least two of the five years before the sale or exchange. Effective for sales and exchanges after October 22, 2004, the residence must have been held for more than five years after the date of acquisition if the property was acquired in a tax-deferred exchange. For example, this would apply if property acquired in a tax-deferred exchange was initially used as rental property and was later converted to a principal residence.

Under the use test, the individual must have occupied the residence as a principal residence for a total of at least two of the five years before the sale or exchange.

The ownership and use tests may be met at different times, provided both tests are met for the five-year period before the sale.

Reduction of "second residence" exclusion/Reduction of exclusion for "nonqualified use" after 2008

Under the rules effective before 2009, a great feature was the ability to convert a residence that was previously a second home, a vacation home or a rental home to a principal residence. Once the home was used more than two years as a principal residence, the exclusion for sale of a principal residence could be claimed for the entire gain up to the exclusion limit ($250,000 or $500,000).

As a revenue raising measure to offset other breaks for homeowners in financial distress, Congress changed this rule in the Housing Assistance Tax Act of 2008, enacted on July 30, 2008 and effective January 1, 2009.[1]

Under the current rule, gain from the sale of a principal residence allocated to a period of nonqualified use will not be eligible for the exclusion. The allocation will be made by making a ratio of the periods of nonqualified use divided by the total period of time the property was owned by the taxpayer.

A period of nonqualified use is a period during which the taxpayer did not use the residence as a principal residence.

Fortunately, under a transitional rule, nonqualified use before January 1, 2009 will be disregarded for this test.

---

1   IRC § 121(b)(4).

There are other exceptions to the rule:

- A period of nonqualified use during the five-year period ending on the date the property is sold that is after the last date the property was used as a principal residence by the taxpayer is disregarded. This should give the taxpayer up to three years to sell the home after moving out without having the exclusion reduced.

- A period of up to 10 years during which the taxpayer or the taxpayer's spouse is serving on "qualified official extended duty" as a member of the armed forces, as a Foreign Service officer, or as an employee of the intelligence community is disregarded. In order to qualify for the extended duty exception, the taxpayer must be stationed at least 50 miles from the taxpayer's principal residence.

- Temporary absences for vacations, traveling on business, etc. won't be considered non-personal use.

- Other periods of temporary absence of up to two years because of a change of employment, health conditions, or other unforeseen circumstances specified by the IRS will be disregarded.

Gain up to the amount of accumulated depreciation for the property remains taxable (at a 25% tax rate) and not eligible for the exclusion.

For example, Jane Taxpayer bought a house for $200,000 on January 1, 2000. She rented the home to tenants from January 1, 2000 to December 31, 2009, and claimed accumulated depreciation deductions of $50,000. On January 1, 2010, she moved into the home and used it as her principal residence until January 2, 2020. Jane sold the home on December 31, 2020 for $400,000.

Nonqualified use before 2009 is disregarded. There were 12 months of nonqualified use during 2009. Nonqualified use from January 2, 2020 to December 31, 2020 is disregarded because it was during the five-year period after moving out of the residence and before the sale. The total months the home was owned was 20 years X 12 = 240.

Here are the results:

Nonqualified use months		12
Total months		/ 240
Nonqualified use ratio		.05

Sales Price		$400,000
Cost	$200,000	
Accumulated depreciation	-50,000	
Adjusted tax basis		-150,000
Total gain		250,000
Accumulated depreciation taxable at 25%		50,000
Other gain		200,000
Nonqualified use amount – not eligible for exclusion $200,000 X .05 (taxable long-term capital gain)		10,000
Gain eligible for exclusion		190,000
Maximum exclusion		-250,000
Remaining gain subject to tax		$ 0

So $10,000 of the gain will be subject to tax as a long-term capital gain (see below about the federal income tax rate for long-term capital gains and see the separate chapter about the 3.8% federal tax for net investment income) and $50,000 accumulated depreciation will be taxed at the 25% rate for depreciation recapture.

Remember that many states don't automatically conform to Federal income tax law changes. You will need to find out if your state has conformed to this rule to determine the state tax consequences of the sale of a principal residence for which there was a period of non-qualifying use.

Ownership and use of prior residences

For principal residences not acquired in a tax-deferred exchange, taxpayers may include the periods of ownership and use of principal residences with respect to which gain was rolled over to the current residence under the old rules.

For example, in 1995 Jack sold a residence he bought in 1980. He replaced the residence under the old rules in 1996. In applying the tests for testing holding periods under the new law, Jack is considered as acquiring the replacement residence in 1980.

Incapacitated taxpayers

A taxpayer who becomes physically or mentally incapable of self-care is deemed to use a residence as a principal residence during the time which the individual owns the residence and resides in a licensed care facility. In order for this exception to apply, the taxpayer must have owned and used the residence as a principal residence for at least one year during the five years before the sale or exchange.

Divorced taxpayers

The ownership and use of a spouse or former spouse are attributed to a taxpayer to whom a residence is transferred incident to a divorce.

Widowed taxpayers

The ownership and use of a deceased spouse are attributed to the surviving spouse.

An unmarried surviving spouse can claim the $500,000 exclusion when the principal residence is sold within two years after the death of his or her spouse and the sale would otherwise qualify.[2] After two years have passed when a surviving spouse sells a residence, he or she will generally only be eligible for the $250,000 exclusion on his or her tax return filed as a single person, head of household or surviving spouse. Since there is usually a basis adjustment to the fair market value of the residence as of the date of death for the decedent's interest in the property (100% for community property owned by married persons or the separate property of the decedent), no tax benefit will be lost unless the residence is the separate property of the surviving spouse.

Married individuals

Married persons filing a joint return will qualify for the $500,000 exclusion on a joint return, provided (1) either spouse meets the ownership test, (2) both spouses meet the use test, and (3) neither spouse is ineligible for exclusion because he or she made a sale or exchange of a residence within the last two years.

Married persons who don't qualify for the $500,000 exclusion may still use the $250,000 exclusion, or a prorated exclusion, if either spouse meets the ownership and use

---

[2] Internal Revenue Code § 121(b)(4).

requirements.

Marriages of legally-married same-sex couples are recognized by the federal government after the Supreme Court's *Windsor* decision in 2013. These couples will now report under the same rules that apply to opposite sex married couples. For details, see your lawyer and tax advisor.

Other joint owners

Unmarried joint owners who otherwise qualify for the exclusion of gain from the sale of a principal residence may each claim a $250,000 exclusion for their share of the gain.[3]

Gain recognized for depreciation

Gain up to the amount of depreciation allowable for the rental or business use of the property after May 6, 1997 will be taxable at a special maximum long-term capital gains rate of 25% and is not eligible for exclusion.

Exclusion prorated

For principal residences except for residences acquired in a tax deferred exchange after October 22, 2004, if a taxpayer does not meet the ownership or residence requirements, a pro-rata amount of the $250,000 or $500,000 exclusion applies if the sale or exchange is due to a change in place of employment, health, or unforeseen circumstances. The amount of the available exclusion is equal to $250,000 ($500,000) multiplied by a fraction equal to the shorter of the number of months of (1) the total of periods during which the ownership and use requirements were met during the five-year period ending on the date of sale, or (2) the period after the date of the most recent sale or exchange to which the exclusion applied divided by 24 months.

For example, Jane had to sell her residence during 2020 because she had to move for a new job. She is a single person. She bought her residence on January 1, 2019 and sold it on January 2, 2020. Her available exclusion is $250,000 X 12 / 24 = $125,000. If Jane realized a gain for the sale of her residence of $100,000, the entire amount would be excluded from her taxable income.

The IRS has issued regulations that explain many alternative scenarios that are eligible for the exclusion prorate. They make it clear that taxpayers who want to upgrade their residence because of an improvement in their economic status do not qualify. Otherwise, the regulations are surprisingly liberal, including allowing taxpayers to prove they are eligible for a hardship exception because of their "facts and circumstances"!

Homeowners in military service, foreign service and federal intelligence

Homeowners in military service, the U.S. Foreign Service, and the federal intelligence community who serve extended duty may qualify for suspension of the holding period rules.

3   Treasury Regulations § 1.121-2(a)(2)

The details are beyond the scope of this book. Please see a qualified tax advisor for details.

Certain expatriates

Nonresident aliens who gave up their US citizenship for the principal purpose of avoiding tax are not eligible for the exclusion.

Involuntary conversions

The destruction, theft, seizure, requisition or condemnation of property is treated as a sale or exchange of the residence. Any gain in excess of the exclusion amount may be deferred by purchasing a replacement residence under the involuntary conversion rules.

It can actually be an advantage to NOT make an involuntary conversion election for replacement property and claim the $250,000 or $500,000 exclusion for insurance proceeds and start the clock running to claim the exclusion again when the home is eventually sold more than two years later.

Losses are generally not deductible

Since a loss from the sale of a principal residence is from the sale of a personal asset, it is not tax deductible.

Repossession by seller

If the seller of a principal residence for which a gain was not recognized under these rules receives a note as part of the sale proceeds and later repossesses the home in satisfaction of the note, and then resells the home within one year after the date of the repossession, the two sales are combined to determine the amount of gain to be excluded from taxable income.[4]

If you have one of these repossessions, I recommend that you get help from a tax advisor who is familiar with these rules.

Federal tax rates on long-term capital gains for individuals

When selling a residence, most homeowners should consult with a professional tax advisor about the consequences of the transaction to avoid an unpleasant surprise on April 15. For example, the owner might have borrowed cash using an equity line of credit secured by the residence and spent the money. When the home is sold, no cash may be received but there could be a taxable gain and income taxes due.

Federal tax rates for long-term capital gains have increased under recent federal tax laws. Under the American Taxpayer Relief Act of 2012 and the Tax Cuts and Jobs Act of 2017, most taxpayers will still be subject to the 15% federal tax rate for long-term capital gains. For 2020, a 20% federal tax rate applies when taxable income exceeds $496,600 for married couples filing a joint return, $248,300 for married persons filing separate returns,

---

4   IRC § 1038(e).

$469,050 for heads of households, and $441,450 for single persons, indexed for inflation in later years. (Note the reduced tax rates under the Tax Cuts and Jobs Act of 2017 are scheduled to expire after 2025.)

The 25% federal tax rate still applies for depreciation recapture relating to real estate.

A separate 3.8% tax on net investment income was adopted in the Patient Protection and Affordable Care Act in 2010. See the separate chapter on that tax. Only the taxable gain from the sale of a principal residence can be subject to the 3.8% net investment income tax. (Note the Patient Protection and Affordable Care Act of 2010 is being contested as unconstitutional. This could result in the 3.8% net investment income tax being eliminated. See your tax advisor for developments.)

Trusts are subject to the 20% federal tax rate for long-term capital gains and the 3.8% net investment income tax when taxable income exceeds $12,950 for 2020. Ouch!

Observations

Now seniors in high tax states, like California, can get a significant exclusion of gain from the sale of their principal residences (the $250,000 and $500,000 exclusion, depending on the state tax laws that apply) and can exclude retirement benefits from their previous state's tax when they move out of state. These are significant incentives to move to a state with no income tax, such as Washington and Nevada.

It is important to keep records of the improvements to your residence and your original escrow when it is likely you will sell the home for an amount over the exclusion amount and for state tax reporting.

For those who would have a substantial taxable gain under the new rules, it may make sense to convert the residence to rental property to be eligible for a tax-deferred exchange.

Remember that a residence that is inherited receives a new "tax basis" (cost to determine gain or loss) equal to the fair market value of the residence as of the date of death of the decedent or the alternate valuation date, if applicable. A residence that is held as community property by married persons is eligible to have the entire basis adjusted. See your tax advisor.

Also remember that the tax basis of a residence that was a replacement residence for a pre-May 7, 1997 sale is reduced for any deferred gain from the previous sale.

An estate or trust does not qualify for the exclusion for the sale of a principal residence. As explained above, there should be little gain provided the sale takes place shortly after death.

The IRS issued rules that are surprisingly liberal for home offices. Although gain must be reported up to the amount of accumulated depreciation for a home office located within the main residence structure, it will otherwise qualify for the exclusion. A home office located in a separate structure from the main residence structure is not eligible for the exclusion. However, a separate structure home office may qualify for a tax-deferred exchange.[5] See your tax advisor for details.

The current rules provide a flexible playing field for real estate investment on a tax-free (or minimal tax) basis.

- At retirement, a taxpayer could sell his or her principal residence, move to his or her vacation home, and sell the former vacation home after two years, qualifying for another exclusion of gain. (But see the new rules reducing this benefit after 2008, explained above.)

- An investor could move into "fix up" homes every two years. The rehabilitated homes could be sold every two years tax free (up to the exclusion amounts)!

- Suppose a taxpayer wants to retire to another location, and has a rental property in addition to a principal residence. The taxpayer could sell the principal residence and claim the exclusion amount. The rental property could be exchanged for another income property in the taxpayer's new location. The replacement rental property could be converted to a principal residence after it has been "aged" to insure the exchange. Then the former rental property could later be sold after the qualifying period of use as a principal residence (more than five years) and the exclusion claimed for the sale. (But see the new rules reducing this benefit after 2008, explained above.)

Your residence may well be "the ultimate tax shelter"! There are significant, legitimate opportunities to be exploited by aggressive taxpayers.

Transferring a family residence to family members at a discount – with two "catches"!

There is an estate planning strategy for transferring a principal residence or vacation home to your children or other beneficiaries at a discounted gift tax value called a qualified personal residence trust, or QPRT.[6] (See below. The advantages have been reduced or eliminated for many families after 2012 and even more so for 2018 - 2025.) There is a big "catch" that makes the strategy suitable for only selected persons – after a stated period of personal use, the property must go to the named beneficiaries. If the person or persons who originally transferred the property continue to use the property, they must pay a fair market rent or lose the benefits of the transfer.

During the stated period of personal use, the property may only be used or available for use by the persons with the retained rights, or their spouse or dependents, as a residence. The property can't be used as a business location, except as a home office, and can't be used

---

5   Rev. Proc. 2005-14.
6   IRC § 2702(a)(3)(ii), Treasury Regulations § 25.2702-5(b)(1).

as temporary lodging for transients, like a "bed and breakfast."

The property is held in a trust that is only permitted to own one residence and cash to pay maintenance expenses. A taxpayer may have a maximum of two QPRTs. The trust is not permitted to sell the property to the previous owners.

Everyone is excited about the arrangement until the stated period of personal use is over. Parents aren't willing to pay rent for the use of "their" home. They are outraged that they might have to repurchase "their" home from their children. That's why I don't favor using this strategy for a principal residence, but recommend it for a second home – usually a vacation home.

A second "catch" is if the transferor/grantor dies before the end of the term of the trust, the entire fair market value of the residence will be included in his or her taxable estate. There is definitely a gamble involved when determining the term of the arrangement!

The qualified personal residence trust is an exception to a rule that the value of a retained interest is disregarded when valuing gifts. The value of a retained interest is computed using a combination of an appraisal and IRS actuarial tables.

In order to qualify, several other requirements must be met that are beyond the scope of this discussion.

The advantages of QPRTs have been reduced or eliminated for most families after 2012 by the American Taxpayer Relief Act of 2012 and even more so by the Tax Cuts and Jobs Act of 2017. The 2012 Act increased the lifetime estate tax exemption to $5,000,000, indexed for inflation after 2010. The Tax Cuts and Jobs Act doubled that exemption to $10,000,000 for 2018 through 2025, indexed for inflation after 2010. The inflation adjusted exemption for 2020 is $11,580,000. Note the exemption is scheduled to revert to $5,000,000, indexed for inflation after 2010, after 2025. In addition, an election is available to make the unused exemption of a deceased spouse available to a surviving spouse, so a married couple could have a combined estate of about $23,160,000 with no federal estate tax. Most U.S. families will have no estate tax. The family receives a tax benefit for the adjustment of the tax basis of the property to fair market value at the date of death when the property is included in a decedent's taxable estate. QPRTs have become a beneficial tax strategy only for very wealthy families.

This is another strategy to include on your checklist of possibilities, but only implement it under the guidance of a qualified attorney.

The temporary increase in the estate and gift tax exemption for 2018 - 2025 creates many unanswered questions for estate planning. See your estate planning attorney to discuss how your estate plan should be updated for them.

For more information, see IRS Publication 523, Selling Your Home, at www.irs.gov.

2
Other Sales of Real Estate

One reason real estate is popular as an investment is that, subject to limitations, ordinary deductions may be claimed for expenses associated with real estate, such as interest expense, property taxes, repairs and maintenance, depreciation, and other operating costs, but the gain from selling real estate may be eligible to be taxed at favorable tax rates for long-term capital gains.

There are also tax-favored ways of selling real estate to postpone the taxation of gains through installment sales and tax-deferred (Section 1031) exchanges, which will be discussed in Chapters 4 and 5.

I apologize in advance for using Internal Revenue Code Section names in this explanation, but they are a short-hand reference that is impossible to avoid when trying to be brief and to the point. Please be patient in "learning tax language" which will be further explained as we progress. I hope the examples make my meaning clear.

Qualifying for favored tax rates

Not all real estate qualifies for favored tax rates.

For example, a developer that builds a group of houses for resale reports the sale of the homes as ordinary income.

An individual who buys homes to fix them up and "quick flip" them also has a trade or business of buying and selling houses, and should report the sales as ordinary business income.

In order to qualify for favored tax rates, the real estate must be held for more than a year and must be held for one of the following purposes: (1) personal use (such as a vacation home); (2) use in a trade or business (such as a commercial building, a motel, a retail store, a factory, a warehouse, or farmland); or (3) investment (such as bare land, or rental houses).

Capital gains and losses

Gains and losses from sales of non-depreciable real estate are generally reported on Schedule D as capital gains and losses. Losses from personal-use real estate, such as a vacation home that hasn't been rented, a second home, unimproved land, or a principal residence, are non-deductible.

When the real estate doesn't have a holding period of more than one year when it is sold, the gain or loss is a short-term capital gain or loss, reported at Part I of Form 8949 and Schedule D. Long-term capital gains and losses (held more than one year) are reported at Part II of Form 8949 and Schedule D. The short-term and long-term amounts are subtotaled, or "netted." If there is a net short-term capital gain for the tax year, it is taxable at ordinary income tax rates, currently up to a 37% maximum federal tax rate for individuals.

Watch the holding period! There's nothing more frustrating than reporting a short-term capital gain from the sale of real estate held exactly one year!

Net short-term capital losses are deducted from net long-term capital gains.

Net long-term capital gains minus net short-term capital losses are currently taxable at a maximum federal tax rate of 20% for individuals. (The federal tax rate on long-term capital gains for corporations ("C corporations") is currently the same as for other taxable income: 21%.)

Net short-term capital losses are added to net long-term capital losses to determine the maximum capital loss deduction for a tax year. The maximum deduction for single persons and married persons filing a joint income tax return is $3,000, $1,500 for married persons filing a separate income tax return. Corporations may only deduct capital losses to the extent of capital gains.

Individuals may carry forward unused capital losses indefinitely (until they die), but may not carry capital losses back. Corporations may carry capital losses back three years and forward five years. Corporations should be especially careful to structure transactions to avoid losing the tax benefit of capital losses.

To see how this works, study Form 8949, Form 1040, Schedule D and Form 1120, Schedule D. You can get a copy of the forms with instructions at www.irs.gov.

Sales of real estate used in a trade or business or for rental

Sales of real estate used in a trade or business are more complex to report than capital gains and losses. There is a special form to report these transactions: Federal Form 4797.

The reason these sales are complex is there are different types of gain that need to be segregated to determine amounts subject to special tax treatment and different tax rates.

Ordinary gains and losses, including sales of real estate used in a trade or business or for rental that haven't been held for more than one year, are reported at Part II of Form 4797.

Most sales of depreciable property are reported at Part III of Form 4797. Note that property that has been held more than one year and sold at a loss is not subject to depreciation recapture or special tax rates applicable under the Section 1245 and Section 1250 explanations below, but is reported with other Section 1231 gains (explained below) at Part I of Form 4797.

Section 1245 gain (ordinary income).

Section 1245 gain is a type of depreciation recapture. Certain amounts previously allowed or allowable as deductions for depreciation are taxable as ordinary income when certain property is sold. This provision mostly applies to sales of personal property, like business equipment or a car. When taxpayers have cost-segregation studies done, a price to be paid for identifying certain improvements as eligible for shorter depreciable lives is having depreciation recapture when those items are sold.

When a taxpayer elects to expense real estate, such as land improvements or qualified improvement property, under Internal Revenue Code Section 179 (see Chapter 7), the amount of the expense deduction is reclassified under Internal Revenue Code Section 1245(a)(3)(C) as Section 1245 depreciation subject to recapture as Section 1245 gain.

A little-known exception for depreciable real estate is commercial property acquired after 1980 and before 1987 for which accelerated depreciation was elected under the Accelerated Cost Recovery System. All of the ACRS depreciation deductions for this property is subject to recapture as ordinary income under Internal Revenue Code Section 1245 and this property is Section 1245 recovery property.[7]

Here's how the recapture works: Jane Taxpayer bought a commercial building for cash in 1981 and elected to depreciate it using an accelerated ACRS method over 15 years. The cost of the building was $100,000 and it is fully depreciated. The cost of the land was $50,000. She sells the property for $500,000 on February 1, 2018.

Sales price		$500,000
Cost of property	$150,000	
Accumulated depreciation	-100,000	
Adjusted tax basis		50,000
Total gain		450,000
Ordinary income for depreciation		
Recapture – Section 1245		100,000
Section 1231 gain – possibly		
long-term capital gain		$350,000

Real estate can also be considered "equipment" when it is an integral part of the manufacturing process, used for bulk storage of commodities (like petroleum), is a single-purpose horticultural structure or is eligible for special tax benefits, such as expensing handicapped improvements. Tax consultants should consult the Internal Revenue Code and regulations for more details.

---

7   IRC Section 1245(a)(5) (Before repeal by the Tax Reform Act of 1986).

Section 1250 property (most depreciable real estate).

Most real estate is depreciated using straight-line methods under the Modified Accelerated Cost Recovery System, and is not subject to recapture at ordinary income tax rates. See Chapter 7.

The accumulated depreciation for real estate that has been depreciated using a straight-line method is "unrecaptured Section 1250 gain." The amount of the gain on the sale, up to the unrecaptured Section 1250 gain, is subject to a federal maximum long-term capital gain rate for individuals of 25%. The amount subject to this rate is shown at line 19 for 2017 Form 1040, Schedule D.

For example, John Taxpayer bought a rental house for cash in 1981. Since the house was residential rental property, it was fully depreciated using the straight-line ACRS method. The amount paid for the building was $30,000 and the amount paid for the land was $10,000. He sells the house on February 1, 2018 for $500,000. (Assume there were no other sales of business property and there was no Section 1231 loss carryover, explained below.)

Sales price		$500,000
Cost	$40,000	
Accumulated depreciation	-30,000	
Adjusted tax basis		10,000
Total Section 1231 gain		490,000
Capital gain taxed at 25% maximum federal rate for "unrecaptured Section 1250 depreciation"		30,000
Capital gain taxed at federal tax rate for long-term capital gains		$460,000

Remember that the depreciation schedule for replacement property received in a tax-deferred exchange or an involuntary conversion may not show the accumulated depreciation for the property surrendered or otherwise replaced with the property on the schedule. The accumulated depreciation for the predecessor property is added to determine the potential "unrecaptured Section 1250 gain," which may be subject to the special 25% federal maximum income tax rate for individuals.

An important real estate-related category is land improvements. (See Chapter 7.) Since land improvements are depreciated at an accelerated rate, the excess of accumulated depreciation over depreciation computed using the straight-line rate is recaptured for them as ordinary income – Section 1250 gain, under Internal Revenue Code Section 1250(a).

If bonus depreciation has been claimed for "qualified improvement property" (see Chapter 7), the lesser of the gain from the sale of the qualified improvement property or the excess of the bonus depreciation over the straight-line depreciation computed using a 15-

year life is taxable as ordinary income under Internal Revenue Code Section 1250(a).

Other special types of real estate.

There are other recapture rules that apply to special types of real estate, such as farm land, mines, and conservation property. These are beyond the scope of this explanation. If they apply to you, it is especially important for to you consult with a tax advisor familiar with these matters.

Section 1231 gains and losses (gains and losses for business property not taxed as depreciation recapture.)

Assets held for more than one year and used in a trade or business or for rental have special tax benefits requiring an intermediate calculation at Part I of Form 4797.

If the total of the gains and losses is a net loss, the loss is deductible as an ordinary loss. It is carried forward to Part II on Form 4797 (line 11 on the 2019 form) and included with the ordinary gain or loss from Form 4797 (line 14 of Form 1040, Schedule 1 for 2019.)

There is a special "recapture" computation for these "Section 1231 losses" to recharacterize net Section 1231 gains for the next five years as ordinary income (to line 8 of 2019 Form 4797.) Any remaining net Section 1231 gains after the recharacterization is taxed as a long-term capital gain and carried to Part II of Schedule D (line 11 of 2019 Form 1040, Schedule D.)

For example, Sam Taxpayer bought a commercial building during 1997 for $500,000 cash. He claimed accumulated straight-line depreciation of $250,000, and sold the property during 2019 for $200,000. He bought a rental home during 2004 for $250,000 cash. He claimed accumulated straight-line depreciation of $125,000 and sold the property during 2020 for $400,000.

2019

Sales price		$200,000
Cost	$500,000	
Accumulated depreciation	-250,000	
Adjusted basis		250,000
Section 1231 (ordinary) loss		-$ 50,000

2020

Sales price		$400,000
Cost	$250,000	
Accumulated depreciation	-125,000	

Adjusted basis	125,000
Section 1231 gain	275,000
Recharacterized to ordinary income for 2019 Section 1231 loss	- 50,000
Total long-term capital gain	225,000
Long-term capital gain taxable at 25% for "unrecaptured Section 1250 depreciation"	125,000
Long-term capital gain taxable at the applicable tax rate	$100,000

(So for 2020, $50,000 of the gain will be taxed as ordinary income, $125,000 will be taxable as a long-term capital gain at the 25% tax rate, and $100,000 will be taxable as a long-term capital gain at the applicable rate, probably 15% or 20%.)

Sale of depreciable property to a related person

Any gain for the sale of depreciable property to a "related person" is taxable as *ordinary income*.[8]

By segregating the amounts for (non-depreciable) land and depreciable improvements, it may be established that most, if not all, of the gain is for the land and qualifies for long-term capital gains rates despite this rule.

Related persons include (1) a seller and corporations, S corporations and partnerships that are controlled directly or indirectly by the seller, (2) a seller and a trust for which the seller or his or her spouse is a beneficiary, and (3) a seller that is an estate and a beneficiary of the estate, unless the sale is in satisfaction of a pecuniary bequest.

Note that family members aren't considered "related persons" for this rule.

There is an exception when the taxpayer can establish to the satisfaction of the IRS that the disposition did not have as one of its principal purposes the avoidance of federal income tax. To satisfy this requirement, the seller would have to apply for a ruling from the IRS.

Selling expenses

Remember that selling expenses, including commissions and transfer taxes, are included in cost or other basis when reporting the sale.

Earnest money deposits

When a cash deposit is made for a sale and the deposit is potentially refundable, the income from the deposit isn't taxable until the sale is closed or the deposit is forfeited to the seller. The deposit that is applied to the sales price of the property is included in the sale proceeds. A forfeited deposit is ordinary income.

---

8   IRC § 1239(a).

Typically earnest money deposits are placed in an escrow account. That is the best approach to avoid arguments with the tax authorities about whether the deposit is currently taxable.

If a seller receives deposit funds and the deposit is non-refundable, the deposit is taxable when received.

Option to purchase

An option is an open offer to buy or sell property during a certain period of time. An option premium is paid for the option privilege. The person who gives the option is called the grantor. The person who receives the option is the grantee. An option is an open contract – it isn't completed until the offer is accepted by exercise.

I am going to focus on an option to purchase in this discussion.

No income is reported by the grantor when an option premium is received.

If the option expires, the grantor reports ordinary income as of the expiration date. If the property would be capital gain property for the grantee, the grantee reports a capital loss. If the property would be trade or business property for the grantee, the grantee reports a Section 1231 loss.[9] If the property would be personal use property for the grantee, like a personal residence, no loss is allowed.[10]

If the option is exercised, the grantor includes the option premium in the sales price of the property. The grantee includes the option premium in the purchase price of the property.

If the grantee sells the option, the holding period is based on the period the grantee held the option. The classification of the gain or loss is based on what the character of the property would have been in the hands of the grantee: Section 1231 gain or loss or capital gain or loss. If the property would have been personal-use property, no loss is allowed.

If the original option provides for an extension (usually for the payment of an additional premium), the extension extends the time at which the option lapses and income is taxable to the grantor. If new terms are negotiated under the extension, the previous option is considered to have lapsed and the income is taxable at the end of the term of the original option.[11]

How to avoid paying tax for personal or investment real estate sales with a "catch" – Charitable Remainder Trusts

For individuals who have an interest in benefiting charities but want to continue to enjoy an income stream from donated properties during their lifetimes, the Charitable

---

9   Treasury Regulations § 1.1234-1(b).
10 Treasury Regulations § 1.1234-1(f).
11 Letter Ruling 9129002.

Remainder Trust (CRT) is an attractive strategy.[12] The "catch" is the principal of the trust will go to a charity and will not be available as a bequest to the surviving family members. That's why a charitable intent is required before going ahead with the strategy.

Appreciated personal or investment real estate may be donated to a Charitable Remainder Trust, and a charitable contribution can be claimed for the donation. Any amount that would be taxable as ordinary income (including certain depreciation recapture) or short-term capital gain if the property was sold will not qualify for deduction as a charitable contribution. (See the section on "Qualifying for favored tax rates" at the beginning of this chapter.) The deduction is limited to 30% of adjusted gross income. Any amount disallowed because of the 30% limit may be carried forward for up to five years.

The donation is reduced for any debt secured by the property, and if the balance of the debt exceeds the tax basis of the property, there will be taxable income for the excess of the debt over the tax basis.

Non-cash donations, such as a gift of real estate to a CRT, require an appraisal as of the date of the donation and are reported on Form 8283. Form 8283 must be included with the donor's income tax return for the year of the donation. If the fair market value of the donated property exceeds $500,000, the appraisal must also be included with the donor's income tax return. The appraisal must be made by a qualified appraiser not earlier than 60 days before the date of the donation, and must be received not later than the due date (including extensions) of the tax return for the year the donation was made.

Since the gift is not completed to the charity because it is held in a CRT, it should be reported on a gift tax return, Form 709, for the year of transfer.

Since a charitable remainder trust is generally tax exempt, the sale of the real estate by the trust will be income tax-free.

The trust is then required to make defined distributions to the person(s) who contributed property. The distributions may be for the lifetime of the donor(s) or other named beneficiary(ies), or for a term of up to 20 years, with the remainder of the trust assets to be distributed to a qualified charity at the termination of the trust. The trust must have a rate of return of at least five percent. The maximum payout of the trust can't exceed 50% of the value of the trust. The value of the charitable remainder (the assets ultimately distributed to the charity) must be at least ten percent of the value of the property transferred to the trust.

There are two kinds of Charitable Remainder Trusts: the Charitable Remainder Annuity Trust (CRAT) and the Charitable Remainder Unitrust (CRUT).

The Charitable Remainder Annuity Trust makes payments of the same fixed amount each year for the term of the trust. The payments are computed based on actuarial tables

---

12   IRC § 664.

provided by the IRS, based on the fair market value of the property when it was contributed to the trust. If the income isn't sufficient to cover the annuity distribution, principal will have to be distributed. Most or all of the distribution amounts will "carry" the trust income to the beneficiary(ies) as taxable income. The income will retain the character of the income to the trust, such as interest or qualified dividends. The advantage of the CRAT to the beneficiaries is certainty of cash flow.

The Charitable Remainder Unitrust pays a fixed percentage of at least five percent of the fair market value of the trust assets to the beneficiary(ies) each year. This means the fair market value of the assets must be re-determined at the beginning of each year. The trust may optionally provide that the distribution is limited to the net income of the trust, with any shortfall to be carried over for a "make up" distribution in a later year. (This is called a NIMCRUT – Net Income with Makeup distributions Charitable Remainder Unitrust.) The distribution "carries" the trust income to beneficiary(ies) as taxable income. The income retains the character of the income to the trust, such as interest or qualified dividends. The advantage of CRUTs is they provide an inflation hedge, since the assets are revalued and the distribution is recomputed each year. They can also provide principal preservation for the trust. Since they require revaluation of assets and recomputation of distributions each year, they are more complex and expensive to operate.

Since the remaining balance of the trust will go to a charity when the trust terminates at death or after the specified term of years, many people who use this strategy replace the value in their estate with life insurance held in an irrevocable life insurance trust.

Charitable Remainder Trusts file an annual income tax return, Form 5227. You can get a copy at www.irs.gov.

You can secure significant tax benefits with a Charitable Remainder Trust, but they are tax-sensitive, requiring a lot of attention in operation. This is only an introduction to the strategy. You should only pursue the strategy under the close guidance of a qualified attorney and a tax consultant to monitor the compliance requirements.

###

For more information, see IRS Publication 544, Sales and Other Dispositions of Assets, at www.irs.gov.

3

Foreclosures, Deeds in Lieu of Foreclosure and Short Sales

The Further Consolidated Appropriations Act of 2020 (H.R. 1865), was enacted on December 20, 2019. One of the provisions extends the exclusion of cancellation of up to $2 million of debt for a principal residence ($1 million for a married person filing a separate return) for one year through 2020. California has not conformed to this extension. Its exclusion expired after 2013. See the details below.

Our nation experienced the effects of tightening mortgage credit after a liberal period. With increases in interest rates for adjustable rate mortgages and the conversion to amortization of principal for interest-only (or negative amortization) loans, home values for homes favored by subprime borrowers (and even other homes) collapsed, and some debtors are still either trying to "walk away" from their homes and allowing them to be foreclosed or are making "short sales."

Real estate values have recovered in many areas with the improving economy, which should alleviate the crisis for many debtors. The values in other areas are recovering more slowly, and property owners in those areas are still suffering.

A "short sale" is selling the home for less than the mortgage balance and trying to get the lender to forgive the unpaid balance. This is a more recent use of the term, and is not the definition for this item in the Internal Revenue Code. In the tax law, a "short sale" is a sale of a borrowed item to be replaced at a future date, usually a security. A case that I know about involving a real estate short sale is a 2008 decision, *Stevens v. Commissioner*.[13] A more recent case is *Simonsen v. Commissioner*, a 2018 decision.[14] With the explosion of real estate short sales, we will undoubtedly soon see more cases with them.

A reason for debtors to consider a "short sale" instead of a foreclosure is to try to protect their credit rating. California has adopted Senate Bill 458, which gives superior anti-deficiency protection for short sales of certain residential real estate compared to trust deed foreclosures. (Laws vary from state to state. Always consult with a real estate attorney relating to continuing liability after a short sale or foreclosure.)

How are foreclosures (and deeds in lieu of foreclosure) taxed?

An important consideration in the results of a foreclosure (or a deed in lieu of foreclosure) is whether the debt is "recourse" or "nonrecourse." If the debt is "recourse,"

---

13   *Stevens v. Commissioner*, T.C. Summary Opinion 2008-61, June 3, 2008.
14   *Simonsen v. Commissioner*, 150 T.C. No. 8, March 14, 2018.

the debtor is personally liable for the debt. If the debt is "nonrecourse," the debt is only secured by the property, and the debtor is not personally liable for the balance.

You should consult with an attorney to determine the status of your mortgage. In California, most mortgages that are used to purchase a residence are nonrecourse, but mortgages from refinancing a previous mortgage before January 1, 2013 are usually recourse. (See "California extends nonrecourse protection when refinancing certain mortgages" below.) You can't always determine whether a mortgage is recourse from the note or paperwork.

When a nonrecourse mortgage is foreclosed, the property is treated as being sold for the balance of the mortgage.[15] This is important because the gain from a foreclosure of a principal residence may be eligible for the $250,000 ($500,000 for jointly-owned marital property) exclusion. (See Chapter 1.)

For example, for foreclosure of a nonrecourse debt,

Nonrecourse debt	$500,000
Tax basis (cost to determine tax gain or loss)	300,000
Gain	$200,000

If the holding period requirements are met and the residence was a principal residence, the above gain would be tax-free.

(Note: The above example is for consistency and contrast with the results for recourse debt. Most non-recourse debt for a residence is purchase-money debt, and would not exceed the tax basis (purchase price) of the residence. When the residence was a replacement residence for a principal residence sold before May 7, 1997, the tax basis can be less than the cost of the residence. Most of the mortgages for residences acquired in that scenario have probably been refinanced and now may be recourse debt.)

For recourse debt, the debt is only satisfied up to the fair market value of the property. There is a sale up to that amount. If the lender forgives the balance of the mortgage, there is *cancellation of debt income,* which is taxed as *ordinary income.*[16] (But see tax relief enacted for certain recourse debt secured by a principal residence, below.)

For example, for foreclosure of a recourse debt,

Recourse debt	$500,000
Fair market value	450,000
Cancellation of debt (ordinary income)	$ 50,000

15	G. Hammel, SCt, 41-1 USTC ¶ 9169.
16	Treasury Regulations § 1.61-12.

(If the cancellation of debt was for "qualified principal residence indebtedness," it will be excluded from taxable income. If the taxpayer still owns the home after the cancellation of debt, the excluded amount will be subtracted from the tax basis of the residence. See the section on "tax relief," below.)

Fair market value	$450,000
Tax basis	300,000
Gain	$150,000

Again, if the holding period requirements are met and the residence was a principal residence the above gain would be tax-free, but the cancellation of debt would generally be taxable as ordinary income, except for certain "qualified principal residence indebtedness." See the section on "tax relief," below.

Tax relief enacted for recourse mortgage on principal residence debt forgiveness (expires after 2021).

Congress passed and President Bush approved H.R. 3648, the "Mortgage Forgiveness Debt Relief Act of 2007." The legislation is effective for discharges of indebtedness on or after January 1, 2007 and before January 1, 2010. The Federal Bailout Legislation, H.R. 1424 passed on October 3, 2008 extended this relief through December 31, 2012. The American Taxpayer Relief Act of 2012, HR 8 passed on January 1, 2013 extended this relief through December 31, 2013. The Tax Increase Prevention Act of 2014, HR 5771, passed on December 19, 2014 extended this relief through December 31, 2014. The Protecting Americans from Tax Hikes (PATH) Act of 2015, enacted on December 18, 2015, extended the relief through December 31, 2016. The Bipartisan Budget Act of 2018, enacted on February 9, 2018, extended the relief through December 31, 2017. The Further Consolidations Appropriations Act of 2020, enacted on December 20, 2019, extended the relief through December 31, 2020.

If Congress doesn't take further action, this relief will expire after 2020.

Under this law, a discharge of "qualified principal residence indebtedness" is excluded from taxable income. "Qualified principal residence indebtedness" is *acquisition indebtedness* secured by the principal residence of a taxpayer as defined for the deduction of residential mortgage interest, but the limit is $2,000,000 for the exclusion ($1,000,000 for the mortgage interest deduction) and $1,000,000 for married persons filing a separate return ($500,000 for the mortgage interest deduction). Also, the exclusion only applies to a mortgage secured by the principal residence of the taxpayer.

The Tax Court expressed confusion about whether a principal residence should be defined the same as for the sale of a principal residence when applying the exclusion for "qualified principal residence indebtedness." (When the residence was owned two out of the five years preceding the sale. See Chapter 1.) In the subject case, the property had been converted from a principal residence to a rental property. The Tax Court avoided ruling on the issue by finding there was no cancellation of indebtedness because the indebtedness was nonrecourse debt, so the cancelled debt was included in the sales proceeds.[17]

For this purpose, acquisition indebtedness is debt incurred to purchase or substantially improve the residence. When a residence is refinanced, any portion of the new mortgage exceeding the acquisition indebtedness doesn't qualify.

The election to exclude the income from discharge of principal residence indebtedness is made on Form 982 (March 2018), Part I, lines 1.e. and 2. The 2019 Form 982 and instructions haven't yet been updated for the extension of the residential mortgage exclusion. According to IRS Publication 4681 for 2017 income tax returns, a basis reduction amount is entered at Part II, line 10.b. only if the taxpayer still owns the residence after the debt cancellation.[18] IRS Publications aren't considered legal authority and I haven't found any other authority for not making a basis adjustment when the debt cancellation happens at the same time as a foreclosure or short sale.

The exclusion does not apply if the discharge relates to providing services to the lender or any other factor not related to a decline in the value of the residence or the financial condition of the taxpayer/borrower.

According to IRS Publication 4681, if the taxpayer continues to own the home after the debt cancellation, the tax basis of the residence (cost used to determine taxable gain or loss on sale) is reduced by any amount of discharge of indebtedness excluded from taxable income, but not below zero. The basis reduction is entered at Part II, Line 10.b. on Form 982. There is no basis adjustment if the debt cancellation happens with a foreclosure or short sale. There will be two calculations: (1) Cancellation of debt income eligible for exclusion and (2) Sale of residence to apply the applicable exclusion.

If the sale of the residence happens after the debt is cancelled, there will be two calculations: (1) Cancellation of debt income eligible for exclusion and (2) Sale of residence to apply the applicable exclusion.

The exclusion of income for discharge of acquisition indebtedness for a principal residence takes precedence over the exclusion relating to insolvency (discussed below), unless the taxpayer elects otherwise.

For example, if the previous example of a foreclosure for a recourse debt was eligible for the exclusion, here are the tax results.

---

17 *Simonsen v. Commissioner*, 150 T.C. No. 8, March 14, 2018.
18 IRS Publication 4681 for 2017 income tax returns, page 10.

Recourse debt	$500,000
Fair market value	450,000
Cancellation of debt excluded from taxable income	$ 50,000
Fair market value	$450,000
Tax basis	300,000
Gain	$150,000

If the holding period requirements are met, the above gain would qualify for the exclusion ($500,000 married, joint or $250,000 single) for sale of a principal residence.

(Remember the foreclosure of a non-recourse mortgage is *not* a discharge of indebtedness, but a "sale" of the residence in satisfaction of the mortgage. Therefore, such a foreclosure won't qualify for the new exclusion, but may qualify for the exclusion of gain for sale of a principal residence. Also, since the balance of acquisition indebtedness is almost always less than the tax basis (cost) of the residence, it would be highly unusual for there to be a gain from a foreclosure.)

Disqualified debt taxable first.

An "ordering rule" in the tax law says that the exclusion only applies to as much of the amount discharged as exceeds the amount of the loan which is not qualified principal residence indebtedness.[19] The IRS explains how to apply the rule at Page 9 of Publication 4681 for 2019 income tax returns.

For example, Julie Smith's residence was foreclosed in 2019. The fair market value of her home was $200,000. The balance of her mortgage was $275,000. Julie had used $50,000 from refinancing her home to pay down her credit card debt, not for home improvements. $50,000 of the debt discharge that is not qualified residence debt would be taxable, and the remaining $25,000 that is qualified residence debt would be excluded from taxable income.

Another example, the residence of John and Mary Taxpayers was foreclosed in 2019. The fair market value of their home was $1,500,000. The balance of their mortgage, which was all acquisition indebtedness, was $2,250,000. Since the maximum qualified principal residence indebtedness is $2,000,000, $250,000 of the debt was not qualified principal residence indebtedness. The $250,000 non-qualified debt cancellation would be taxable income, and the remaining $500,000 that is qualified canceled indebtedness would be excluded from taxable income.

Amounts that are otherwise taxable in the above examples could qualify for exclusions under other exceptions, such as for insolvency or bankruptcy.

---

19 Internal Revenue Code § 108(h)(4).

California debt cancellation tax relief for homeowners (expired December 31, 2013)

California also enacted relief legislation for cancellation of mortgage debt relating to the acquisition of a principal residence

California hasn't yet conformed to the effective date for its exclusion to the December 31, 2016 federal expiration date, and the limit for its exclusion is much lower than the federal exclusion.

Governor Brown vetoed AB 99 (Perea), which would have extended California's partial conformity to the exclusion for cancellation of debt for a principal residence through December 31, 2014 on October 10, 2015. It seems unlikely that another extension bill will be enacted.

Governor Brown signed AB 1393, extending the California exclusion through December 31, 2013 on July 21, 2014.

Governor Schwartzenegger signed SB 401(Wolk), the Conformity Act of 2010, on April 12, 2010.

Effective for taxable years 2009 through 2013, the maximum qualified principal residence indebtedness eligible for relief is $400,000 for taxpayers who file as married or registered domestic partners filing a separate return and $800,000 for taxpayers who file joint returns, single persons, heads of household and qualifying widows or widowers (other individual taxpayers). The federal limits are $1 million for married persons filing a separate income tax return or $2 million for other individual taxpayers.

The debt relief that can be excluded from taxable income is limited to $250,000 for married or registered domestic partners filing a separate return and $500,000 for other individual taxpayers. The federal exclusion is limited to the amount of qualified principal residence indebtedness.

Note that the amount that could be excluded from taxable income for California for 2009 through 2013 was increased compared to the amounts that could be excluded for 2007 or 2008, which was $125,000 for married or registered domestic partners filing a separate return and $250,000 for other individual taxpayers.

There is no California equivalent to Form 982, Reduction of Tax Attributes Due to Discharge of Indebtedness. Use the federal form marked "California" at the top.

Remember the tax basis of the residence is reduced for the excluded gain.

What happens with a "short sale"?

Short sales are taxed under the same rules as foreclosures.

Recourse debt cancellation is not satisfied with the surrender of the property, so any debt not satisfied with the sale proceeds would be taxable as cancellation of debt income, except for certain "qualified principal residence indebtedness." See section on "tax relief," above.[20]

Therefore, the tax consequences would be similar to the "recourse debt" example, above. The buyer and seller might also have legal concerns about whether the lender would consent to the transaction and whether (for recourse debt) the lender would in fact forgive the debt.

For example, for a recourse debt short sale,

Net sale proceeds	$450,000
Tax basis	300,000
Gain	$150,000
Debt	$500,000
Pay off using net sale proceeds	450,000
Cancellation of debt (ordinary income)	$ 50,000

(If the cancellation of debt was for "qualified principal residence indebtedness," it will be excluded from taxable income and be subtracted from the tax basis of the residence. See the section on "tax relief," above.)

For non-recourse debt short sales *when the seller and buyer require the cancellation of the debt by the lender as a condition of the sale*, the debt cancellation is included in the sale proceeds, like for a foreclosure.[21]

Therefore, a "short sale" can be a viable alternative to a foreclosure for debtors with nonrecourse debt and who qualify for the exclusion from income of the gain from the sale of a principal residence.

What about selling expenses for a recourse mortgage?

For simplicity, I have disregarded selling expenses in the above discussion. For a short sale, selling expenses reduce the sales proceeds available to reduce the loan. For a foreclosure or deed in lieu of foreclosure, selling expenses are added to the debt.[22] The net result should be similar, assuming the fair market value of the property equals the selling price for a short sale.

---

20 Rev. Rul. 92-99, 1992-2 CB 518. Also see Treasury Regulations Section 1.1001-2(a)(2).
21 *Briarpark v. Commissioner*, 5th Circuit, 99-1 US Tax Cases 99-1 ¶ 50,209, 1/6/1999; T.C. Memo 1997-298, 6/30/1997. Also see Treasury Regulations Section 1.1001-2. (Thanks to Richard Ogg, EA, who brought the *Briarpark* decision to my attention!) *Simonsen v. Commissioner*, 150 T.C. No. 8, March 14, 2018.
22 *Jerry Myers Johnson v. Commissioner*, TC Memo 1999-162, affirmed CA-4, 2001-1 USTC ¶ 50,391.

For example, for foreclosure of a recourse debt,

Recourse mortgage balance	$500,000
Selling expenses	50,000
Total debt	$550,000
Fair market value	450,000
Cancellation of debt (ordinary income)	$100,000

(If the cancellation of debt was for "qualified principal residence indebtedness," it will be excluded from taxable income. According to IRS Publication 4681, if the cancellation of indebtedness happened relating to a short sale, no basis adjustment would be required. If the taxpayer still owned the home after the debt cancellation, the exclusion amount would be subtracted from the tax basis of the residence. See the section on "tax relief," above.)

For example, for a recourse debt short sale,

Sales price	$450,000
Selling expenses	-50,000
Tax basis	-300,000
Gain	$100,000
Recourse mortgage balance	$500,000
Pay off using net sale proceeds ($450,000 sales price - $50,000 selling expenses)	400,000
Cancellation of debt (ordinary income)	$100,000

(Same caveat for "qualified principal residence indebtedness" as above.)

Other exceptions for cancellation of debt income

Cancellation of debt income may not be taxable if the debtor is insolvent or has the debt discharged in bankruptcy. [23] With recent changes in the federal bankruptcy laws, it is much harder for individuals to file bankruptcy than before the changes.

What if the fair market value of the home has dropped after purchase?

Example - Non-recourse foreclosure/short sale

Mortgage balance	$500,000
Tax basis	700,000

---

23   IRC Sections 108(a)(1)(A) and 108(a)(1)(B).

Loss	-$200,000

(The fair market value of the property is disregarded for a non-recourse mortgage.)

If this is a principal residence, the loss is a non-deductible personal loss.

Example – Recourse foreclosure/short sale

Mortgage balance	$500,000
Fair market value	450,000
Cancellation of debt income	$ 50,000

(But see the rules for exclusion for cancellation of "qualified principal residence indebtedness" in the section on "tax relief," above.)

Fair market value	$450,000
Tax basis	700,000
Loss (for personal residence, non-deductible)	-$250,000

Considerations for rental real estate

Owners of rental properties often have accumulated suspended passive activity losses that can be applied against the income from a debt cancellation with respect to the rental.

Losses from the sale of income-producing properties may be deductible as ordinary losses under Internal Revenue Code Section 1231. (The loss is reported on Form 4797.) The loss may offset cancellation of debt income. If the property isn't income producing, the loss may be a capital loss, limited to capital gains plus $3,000.

Taxpayers other than C corporations may elect to exclude cancellation of "qualified real property business indebtedness" from taxable income.[24] This is mostly debt incurred to acquire, construct, reconstruct or substantially improve real property used in a trade or business. The IRS Chief Counsel has said that rental real estate is considered to be used in a trade or business provided the taxpayer didn't use the property for more than 14 days in the taxable year.[25] Refinanced debt up to the qualifying amount of a previous debt also qualifies. The tax basis of depreciable real property is reduced for the excluded gain. The amount excluded is limited to the adjusted basis of depreciable real property before the discharge.

Exclusions for discharges of debt in bankruptcy in a title 11 case and up to the amount of insolvency are also available for cancellations of debt relating to investment real estate.

---

24 Internal Revenue Code Sections 108(a)(1)(D) and 108(c).
25 CCA 200919035, February 20, 2009.

The tax basis of assets must be reduced for the excluded gain.

California liability relief for Short Sales

California enacted SB 458, on July 11, 2011. Under this legislation, when a short sale is made of a California dwelling with not more than four units with the written consent of the holders of the deeds of trust or mortgage for the first deed of trust and junior mortgages, the lenders may not pursue the seller of the property for any deficiency on the mortgages.

In order to qualify for this relief, the seller must meet two requirements: (1) Title must be voluntarily transferred to a buyer by grant deed or by other document of conveyance that has been recorded in the county where all or part of the real property is located; and (2) The proceeds of the sale must be tendered to the mortgagee, beneficiary, or the agent of the mortgagee or beneficiary, in accordance with the parties' agreement.

A holder of a note may not require the trustor, mortgagor or maker of the note to pay any additional compensation, aside from the proceeds of the sale, in exchange for the written consent to the sale. (The seller isn't prohibited from *offering* a partial payment to a mortgage holder to get consent, but the *seller* must initiate the offer.)

The liability relief for short sales is superior protection compared to trust deed foreclosures for recourse mortgages. For a recourse mortgage, the anti-deficiency protection only applies to the first trust deed when that mortgage is foreclosed.

A short sale gives the property owner more control over the process than a trust deed foreclosure.

Since the lender doesn't have to consent to the short sale and has the option of pursuing a "long form" judicial mortgage foreclosure, including the ability to pursue deficiencies, it appears most California mortgages for residences other than for the original purchase of a principal residence will still be recourse loans when refinancing was done before January 1, 2013. (Judicial foreclosures are very rare in California for residential real estate. But see below when refinancing was done after December 31, 2012.)

The legislation is a two-edged sword. More lenders might not consent to short sales since they are foregoing significant legal rights.

California extends nonrecourse protection when refinancing certain mortgages

Governor Brown approved Senate Bill 1069 on July 9, 2012. Effective January 1, 2013, a refinancing for a California dwelling for not more than four families occupied entirely or in part by the purchaser will still be nonrecourse for the portion of the loan principal refinanced that was a purchase money mortgage.

For example, Sally Smith bought a home in 2010 for $500,000, for which she borrowed $400,000 on a mortgage secured by the home. On February 1, 2013, she refinances the mortgage, with a current balance of $395,000, and replaces it with a new mortgage for $450,000. $395,000 of the new mortgage is nonrecourse, and $55,000 of the new mortgage is recourse.

"Nonrecourse" means the lender can only look to the residence for recovery of the principal in the event of default. See the section "How are foreclosures (and deeds in lieu of foreclosure) taxed?" about the tax consequences of a foreclosure or short sale with a non-recourse mortgage.

It's unclear whether the new rule will apply for subsequent refinancings or can only be applied once.

We recommend that you always consult with a real estate attorney when planning a short sale or foreclosure. You also might want to consult with an attorney about whether refinancing will result in a mortgage that is nonrecourse.

The legal rules for short sales and foreclosures are complex. You should always consult with a real estate attorney for a short sale or foreclosure.

For more information, there are explanations about foreclosures and cancellation of debt in IRS Publications 523, Selling Your Home; 552, Taxable and Nontaxable Income; and 544, Sales and Other Dispositions of Assets at www.irs.gov. Also see IRS Publication 4681, Canceled Debts, Foreclosures, Repossessions and Abandonments.

4

Installment Sales

What is an installment sale?

An installment sale is a disposition of property where at least one payment is to be received after the close of the taxable year in which the disposition occurs.

Planning benefits of installment sales

Installment sales are a powerful tool in the real estate tax planning arsenal. Here are five ways that installment sales can be used to your advantage: (1) a seller postpones paying tax on a portion of the taxable gain from selling property until cash is collected, roughly matching the requirement to pay income taxes with the receipt of cash; (2) interest income can be collected on amounts that otherwise would have been paid as taxes; (3) an installment sale to a family member is an effective way to "freeze" the value of an asset for estate planning and income-shifting, (4) you might be able to keep your taxable income below the thresholds where the federal income tax rate for long-term capital gains increases from 15% to 20%, (5) by spreading gain over several years, a seller might be able to keep his or her income below the adjusted gross income thresholds of the net investment income tax. (See chapter 14.)

Certain items treated as cash received in the year of sale

Notes payable on demand and bonds that are readily tradable on a securities market that are received as consideration for a sale of real estate are treated as cash when received.[26]

What property isn't eligible for installment sale reporting?

Inventorial personal property isn't eligible for installment sale reporting. This applies to businesses that sell products. For example, a department store can't report merchandise sales for which it carries open accounts receivable from customers using the installment method.

Sales of marketable securities aren't eligible for installment sale reporting.

More pertinent to real estate sales, "dealer dispositions" don't qualify. A dealer disposition of real property is any disposition of real property which is held by the taxpayer for sale to customers in the ordinary course of the taxpayer's trade or business. For example, sales of homes in a housing development don't qualify for installment sale reporting. If a taxpayer regularly buys "fixer upper" homes, rehabilitates them and sells them without renting them for a period of time, he or she probably has a trade or business of rehabilitating homes and will not be eligible for installment sale reporting. Quick sale or "wholesale flipping" of houses usually won't qualify for installment sale reporting.

---

26   IRC § 453(f)(4).

There are exceptions to "dealer disposition" sales for property used or produced in the trade or business of farming and for timeshares and residential lots. There is an interest charge paid to the IRS for these sales.[27] The interest is shown as an additional tax on the income tax return, but may be eligible for a tax deduction as interest expense.[28]

How is the election made?

If real estate or a casual sale of personal property is made with a payment received after the year of sale, installment sale reporting applies by default. A taxpayer may elect not to report an installment sale using the installment method. The election out is made by reporting the full amount of the selling price, including the face amount of the installment obligation, on the tax return filed for the taxable year in which the installment sale occurs filed on or before the due date, including extensions, of the taxpayer's tax return for that taxable year.

Late elections or revocations of elections are only permitted with the consent of the IRS.

Installment sales are reported on Federal Form 6252. You can get a copy at www.irs.gov.

Why elect to not use the installment method?

Here are two reasons that come to mind for not reporting using the installment method: (1) The taxpayer has capital losses to partially or completely eliminate the capital gain; (2) Tax rates could be higher in the future. If you report using the installment method, the future reported income could be subject to higher tax rates, resulting in paying more income taxes on the income (a gamble).

Ordinary income from depreciation recapture isn't eligible for installment sale reporting

Ordinary income from depreciation recapture, principally under Internal Revenue Code Section 1245 (see Chapter 2, Other sales of real property), is not eligible for installment sale reporting.[29] This income is taxable in the year of sale. It is entered at line 12 on 2019 Form 6252 (Installment Sale Income). Any additional section 1231 gain or capital gain is eligible for installment sale reporting.

Income subject to highest rate is taxed first

Section 1231 gains and losses from installment sales of business or rental property are netted on 2019 Form 4797, line 4. If a net gain results and any nonrecaptured Section 1231 losses from prior years at line 8 don't recharacterize the balance of the gain to ordinary

---

27   IRC § 453(l)(3).
28   IRC § 453(l)(3)(C).
29   IRC Section 453(i).

income, the balance is carried forward (for individuals) to line 11 on 2019 Schedule D.

A computation is made on the Unrecaptured Section 1250 Gain Worksheet in the instructions for 2019 Schedule D to determine if any of the gain is subject to the special 25% tax rate for long-term capital gains.[30] This computation will result in the long-term capital gain subject to the 25% special tax rate being taxed first. The amount subject to the special rate from the Worksheet is carried to line 19 of Schedule D.[31]

How the taxable gain is computed each year

In order to determine the amount of gain to report each year, a ratio is computed, called the gross profit percentage. The gross profit percentage is the gross profit (gain eligible for installment sale reporting) divided by the contract price.

The contract price is the sales price (line 5 of 2019 Form 6252) minus the mortgages and liabilities of the seller that the buyer has either assumed or taken the property under the terms of the sale (line 6 of 2019 Form 6252), plus the excess of those mortgages and liabilities over the adjusted basis of the property, including the depreciation recapture taxed in the year of sale and the expenses of the sale (line 13 of 2019 Form 6252). The excess is indicated at line 17 of 2019 Form 6252. The contract price is indicated at line 18 of (2019) Form 6252 for the year of sale.

The excess of the mortgages and debts assumed in excess of basis, etc. (line 17 of 2019 Form 6252) is treated as a payment received in the year of the sale (line 20 of 2019 Form 6252).

This gross profit ratio is applied as payments are received each year for the installment sale to determine the amount of gain reported each year.

Wrap around mortgages

A way to further postpone the tax on an installment sale is to have a *wrap around mortgage*. The buyer does not assume the mortgage balance and debts of the seller or take the property "subject to" those debts. The buyer gives the seller cash plus a mortgage for the entire selling price, and the seller remains personally liable for and responsible for making the payments for the previously-existing mortgage and debts. Therefore, the excess of the mortgage and liabilities over the tax basis plus ordinary income plus selling expenses will not be treated as a payment in the year of sale.

Most lenders prohibit wrap-around mortgages in their mortgage terms, and can accelerate the payoff of the mortgage if this requirement is violated.

The Tax Court has ruled that a purchaser is deemed to assume the seller's debt and a wrap around may fail when the purchaser is directly obligated to the mortgagee as a guarantor of payment and could have had an action brought directly against him by the

---

30   2017 Schedule D instructions, page D-13.
31   Treasury Regulations § 1.453-12(a).

mortgagee without any prior efforts at collection from the seller.[32]

The IRS doesn't like wrap around mortgages, but lost a case, *Professional Equities, Inc. v. Commissioner* (89 T.C. 165, July 23, 1987) and has acquiesced to that decision. It has not updated its regulations for this change.

Example with and without a wrap around mortgage

Without - Jane Seller sold a commercial building in 20X1 for $3,000,000. The buyer assumed the $2,000,000 mortgage, paid $100,000 cash down and gave Jane a second mortgage of $900,000 for the balance of the purchase price. Jane bought the building in 1990 for $2,000,000 and has claimed accumulated (straight-line) depreciation of $900,000. Selling expenses are $120,000. In 20X2, Jane received a $100,000 principal payment on the second mortgage. This is Jane's only sale of business property for 20X1 and 20X2.

With – Same facts as "without," except the buyer did not assume the $2,000,000 mortgage. Jane remains responsible for making the mortgage payments on the $2,000,000 mortgage. Jane receives $100,000 cash down plus a second mortgage of $2,900,000 for the purchase price. In 20X2, Jane received a $300,000 principal payment on the second mortgage.

Taxable income for 20X1

	Without (Assumed debt)	With (Wraparound)
Mortgage assumed	$2,000,000	
Cost (tax basis)	2,000,000	
Accumulated depreciation	-900,000	
Depreciation recapture	0	
Selling expenses	120,000	
Subtotal	1,220,000	
Excess of mortgage assumed over adjusted tax basis plus depreciation recapture plus selling expenses	$ 780,000	
Selling price	$3,000,000	$3,000,000
Cost	2,000,000	2,000,000
Accumulated depreciation	-900,000	-900,000
Depreciation recapture	0	0
Selling expenses	120,000	120,000
Subtotal	1,220,000	1,220,000
Gross profit	$1,780,000	$1,780,000

[32]   F.J. *Voight*, 68 TC 99, Affirmed CA-5, 80-1 USTC ¶ 9310, 614 F2d 94.

Selling price	$3,000,000	$3,000,000
Less mortgage assumed	-2,000,000	
Plus excess of mortgage assumed treated as payment in year of sale	780,000	
Contract price	$1,780,000	$3,000,000
Gross profit percentage (gross profit / contract price)	100.000%	59.333%
Unrecaptured Section 1250 gain – lesser of gross profit or accumulated depreciation	$900,000	$900,000

Taxable income for 20X1

Excess mortgage assumed	$780,000	
Cash down payment	100,000	$100,000
Total payments received	880,000	100,000
Gross profit percentage	X 100.00%	X 59.33%
Taxable Section 1231 gain	$880,000	$59,333

Since the gain is less than the unrecaptured Section 1250 gain, it is taxable as a long-term capital gain at a 25% maximum federal tax rate.

Taxable income for 20X2

	Without (Assumed debt)	With (Wraparound)
Cash payments received	$100,000	$300,000
Gross profit percentage	X 100.000%	X 59.333%
Taxable Section 1231 gain	$100,000	$177,999
Total unrecaptured Section 1250 gain	$900,000	$900,000
Less amount taxed in 20X1	-880,000	-59,333
Untaxed balance at beginning of 20X2	$20,000	$840,667

Long-term capital gain taxable at 25% maximum federal tax rate (lesser of untaxed balance of unrecaptured

Section 1250 gain and taxable Section 1231 gain)	$20,000	$177,999
Long-term capital gain taxable at the federal tax rate for long-term capital gains (usually 15% or 20%.) (balance)	$80,000	$0

Like-kind exchanges

See Chapter 5.

Some like-kind exchanges may have taxable income because unlike property, or "boot," is received as part of the consideration in the exchange. If part of the boot is an installment note, the taxable gain may be reported using the installment sale method. [33]

The gross profit for the exchange is determined based on the rules for like-kind exchanges, so taxable income will be the lesser of the realized gain or the "boot" received. The deferred gain is excluded from the gross profit. Boot will usually be cash plus notes. There may be other "unlike" property involved if there is a cost segregation study. (See Chapter 7.)

Like-kind property received is excluded from the contract price.

For example, Jane Taxpayer exchanges her building during 20X1 for land worth $800,000, $200,000 cash and a $500,000 installment note. There is no debt balance for the building. She bought the building in 1999 for $800,000, and has accumulated depreciation of $200,000. Jane has no other gains and losses for 20X1.

Realized gain		
Land	$ 800,000	
Cash	200,000	
Note	500,000	
Amount received		$1,500,000
Cost basis	$ 800,000	
Accumulated depreciation	200,000	
Adjusted tax basis		600,000
Realized gain		$ 900,000
"Boot" received		
Cash	$200,000	

---

[33] IRC § 453(f)(6).

Note	500,000	
Total boot		$ 700,000
Recognized gain/gross profit		$ 700,000
Contract price		
Amount received	$1,500,000	
Less like-kind property	-800,000	
Contract price		$ 700,000
Gross profit percentage –		
Gross profit / Contract price		100.000%
Cash received in year of sale, 20X1		$200,000
X Gross profit percentage		X 100.000%
Taxable Section 1231 gain for 20X1		$200,000
Unrecaptured Section 1250 gain		$200,000
Long-term capital gain taxable at 25% (lesser of taxable 1231 gain and Unrecaptured Section 1250 gain)		$200,000

Sale of principal residence

In some cases, the gain from the sale of a principal residence may exceed the exclusion amount. (See Chapter 1 on Sale of Principal Residence.)

If the seller takes a note back as part of the sales proceeds, the taxable income may be reported using the installment method.

We may see more of these "creative financing" transactions by individuals seeking enhanced interest returns and avoiding volatile securities investments.

Mixed property sales

A single sale of mixed property under one contract is a sale of the individual assets and must be broken down to separate components. For example, a sale of business assets may include a sale of depreciable equipment, inventory and a commercial building. The separate items must be identified and the sales price must be prorated based on the values of the various assets.[34]

---

34   Revenue Ruling 55-79.

Some of the items might qualify for installment sale reporting (land and structural components of the commercial building) and others might not (inventory, depreciable equipment if all of the gain is depreciation recapture.)

Insufficient or unstated interest for installment sale note

Interest income is taxed as ordinary income at regular federal income tax rates up to 37%, effective 2019, and long-term capital gains are taxed at more favorable tax rates, 25% for "unrecaptured Section 1250 gain" and up to 20% for other long-term capital gains. The 3.8% federal surtax on net investment income can also apply to interest income and certain capital gains. (See chapter 14.)

Sellers may try to reduce their income tax bills by increasing the sale price and having reduced or no interest on the installment sale note.

Congress has insured that at least a minimum amount of the loan proceeds are taxed as interest by creating imputed interest rules.[35]

To determine if there is unstated interest, a computation is made to discount payments over the term of the contract at "applicable federal rates,"[36] which are published by the IRS each month. If the discounted amount is less than the stated sales price, part of the sales price is recharacterized as interest. For a sale or exchange, the applicable federal rate is the lowest of the rates published for the three-calendar-month period ending with the calendar month in which there is a binding contract in writing for the sale or exchange.

The maximum interest rate for this computation for a sale of land with a sale price up to $500,000 to certain related parties is 6%.

Rather than go through the gyrations of making these computations, I recommend that you be sure there is adequate stated interest on your contract by consulting with a tax advisor or looking up the applicable federal rates at the IRS web site, www.irs.gov.

Interest charge due to IRS for some installment sales

Congress recognized that installment sales represented a type of interest-free loan from the U.S. government to taxpayers in the form of postponed payment of income taxes. As part of its budget-balancing process, it adopted an interest charge for deferred taxes on certain non-dealer installment sales.[37] (See below for an interest charge for dealers.)

The interest charge only applies when the sales price of the property exceeds $150,000. In addition, the interest charge will only apply when the face amount of all installment sale notes for the year of sale and outstanding at the end of a taxable year exceed $5,000,000.

---

35   IRC § 483.
36   IRC § 1274(d).
37   IRC § 453A.

In applying this test, all persons treated as a single employer are treated as one person. This would usually apply to groups of controlled corporations.

Each member of a married couple who file a joint income tax return is entitled to a separate $5,000,000 limitation, so if the couple owns property sold as joint tenants of community property, they can have a total of up to $10,000,000 of uncollected proceeds at the end of taxable year and not be subject to the interest charge.[38]

In addition, installment sales of personal use property for the seller (like a personal residence or a second home) or of property used or produced in the trade or business of farming are not subject to the interest charge.

The interest for a taxable year is computed by multiplying the interest rate for underpayments of income tax as of the end of the tax year (3% for 2020) times the portion of the deferred tax attributable for installment sale obligations over $5,000,000.

For example, Jane Taxpayer had a $6,000,000 balance receivable for an installment sale of land formerly held for investment as of the end of 2020. The gross profit percentage was 16.66667%.

Her interest charge for 2020 was:

Balance of installment sale obligations Receivable		$6,000,000
Gross profit percentage		16.66667%
Total deferred income		$1,000,002
Excess of balance over $5,000,000	$1,000,000	
Divided by total balance	/ $6,000,000	
Percentage excess		16.666%
Deferred income for excess of installment sale obligations receivable over $5,000,000		166,660
Maximum tax rate for long-term capital gains		20%
Tax on applicable deferred income		33,332
Underpayment penalty rate		3%
Interest charge		$1,000

---

38   Technical Advice Memorandum 9853002, January 4, 1999.

The interest charge may be deductible as interest expense for interest paid or accrued during a taxable year if it's a business expense or investment interest expense.

Repossessions

The gain or loss recognized when the property is repossessed is the amount of money and fair market value of any property other than the debt of the purchaser received as payment on the property before the repossession minus the gain previously reported as income.[39]

The gain from repossessing the property is limited to the untaxed installment sale gain less costs of repossession. The character of the gain is the same as for the installment sale.

The tax basis of the repossessed property is the tax basis of the installment note plus any taxable gain relating to the repossession and costs of repossession.

For example, John Taxpayer sold a commercial building for $2,000,000 during 20X1. He received $200,000 cash and a note for $1,800,000. The gain for the sale was $500,000. After 20X1, he received $200,000 of principal payments, leaving a principal balance of $1,600,000. During 20X4, he repossessed the building, incurring $40,000 of costs for the repossession.

The gross profit percentage is $500,000 / $2,000,000 = 25%.

The untaxed gain is:

Total gain		$500,000
Cash down payment	$200,000	
Principal payments received	200,000	
Total cash received	400,000	
Gross profit percentage	25%	
Taxed gain		100,000
Untaxed gain		$400,000
Total cash received before repossession		$400,000
Less gain previously taxed		-100,000

---

39 IRC § 1038.

Potential gain from repossession	$300,000
Limitation	
Untaxed installment sale gain	$400,000
Less costs of repossession	-40,000
Limitation	$360,000
Taxable gain – lesser of potential gain or limitation	$300,000
Tax basis of repossessed property:	
Balance of installment sale note at repossession	$1,600,000
Untaxed gain balance	
at repossession	$400,000
Taxed gain at repossession	-300,000
Minus untaxed gain	-100,000
Add costs of repossession	40,000
Tax basis of repossessed property	$1,540,000

Sales to related persons who resell the property

If an installment sale is made to a "related person" and that person resells the property within two years after the close of the sale and the installment sale hasn't already been paid off, then the balance of the installment sale loan is deemed to be paid off and any previously untaxed gain becomes currently taxable.[40]

If there is an offsetting option or short sale for the related person that reduces the risk of ownership, the two-year holding period is suspended, and the time a resale will trigger the remaining gain is extended.

Related persons include partnerships, corporations and S corporations controlled directly or indirectly by the seller, estates and trusts for the benefit of the seller, and most family members, except cousins, uncles and aunts. If there will be a resale of the property within two years of an installment sale, the seller should review this issue with his or her tax advisor.

For example, John Taxpayer sells land to his son, James Taxpayer in 20X1. The sale is reported as an installment sale. James resells the property during 20X2 to Jane Smith,

---

40   IRC § 453(e).

an unrelated person, when John has previously unreported capital gain of $200,000. Jane assumes the note payable to John for the purchase of the property. John will have to report the $200,000 as taxable income for 20X2, even though James hasn't paid off the note payable to John for the purchase of the property.

There are exceptions to this rule when there is an involuntary conversion of the real estate (usually as a result of a casualty or condemnation) or when the property is sold after the death of the seller or the buyer in the installment sale. There is another exception to the rule when the taxpayers can establish to the satisfaction of the IRS tax avoidance was not a principal purpose of the first or second sale, which would require requesting a ruling from the IRS.

Sale of depreciable property to a related person

Installment sale reporting is generally disallowed when depreciable property is sold to a related person.[41] In addition, any gain for the sale of depreciable property is taxable as *ordinary income*.[42]

By segregating the amounts for (non-depreciable) land and depreciable improvements, it may be established that most, if not all, of the gain is for the land and qualifies for installment sale reporting despite this rule.

Related persons include corporations, S corporations and partnerships that are controlled, directly or indirectly by the seller, a trust for which the taxpayer or his or her spouse is a beneficiary, and the executor and a beneficiary of an estate, unless the sale is in satisfaction of a pecuniary bequest.

Note that family members aren't considered "related persons" for this rule.

There is an exception when the taxpayer can establish to the satisfaction of the IRS that the disposition did not have as one of its principal purposes the avoidance of federal income tax. To satisfy this requirement, the seller would have to apply for a ruling from the IRS.

Borrowing with installment sale note used as security

If a taxpayer who isn't a dealer borrows money and pledges an installment note as security for the loan, the lesser of the balance of the installment sale note or the amount of cash received from the loan will be treated as a payment for the installment sale. The amount is considered received on the later of the time the loan becomes a secured indebtedness or the time the proceeds of the loan are received by the seller.[43]

A payment is treated as secured by an interest in the installment sale note to the extent the arrangement allows the seller to satisfy all or a portion of the indebtedness with the installment sale note.

---

41   IRC § 453(g).
42   IRC § 1239(a).
43   IRC § 453A(d).

Contingent payment sales

Some sales are structured so the total selling price can't be determined at the close of the taxable year of sale. Such sales can be reported using the installment sale method. In some cases, the arrangement may be considered as retaining a partnership or joint venture interest in the property sold, or as the uncertain amount being classified as interest income. Sales contracts stated in foreign currency are also considered to be contingent payment sales.[44]

These transactions require recomputations of gain and interest during the term of the contract. The details of the tax rules for these transactions are beyond the scope of this discussion. Consult with a tax advisor.

Interest charge for sales by dealers of timeshares and residential lots

The only sales by dealers that qualify for installment sale reporting are sales of timeshares, residential lots, and farm property. Since these are dealer sales, the income reported will be ordinary income. When dealers elect to report sales of timeshares and residential lots using the installment method, they agree to pay an interest charge for the deferred tax.[45]

The timeshare rights are for use of residential real property for not more than six weeks per year, or a right to use specified campgrounds for recreational purposes. Family rights of spouses, children, grandchildren and parents are aggregated for this test.

The interest charge is paid to the IRS as the payments are received. The tax attributable to the installment sale payments received is computed, and interest is computed based on the period from the date of sale to the date the payment is received. The interest rate is the applicable federal rate (AFR) under Internal Revenue Code Section 1274 for the date of sale, compounded semiannually. The IRS publishes these applicable federal rates each month. Only the rate for the month of sale applies; a special rule that would otherwise allow the lowest rate for the 3-month period ending with the month of the contract doesn't apply.

No interest applies for payments received in the year of sale.

For example, XYZ Land Company (a C corporation) sells residential lots. XYZ Land had taxable income of $100,000 for principal payments received on November 1, 2019 for installment sales of land on November 1, 2009. The installment notes were for 10 years.

The tax for the collections was	
$100,000 X 21% tax rate	$21,000

44	Treasury Regulations § 15A.453-1(c).
45	IRC § 453(l)(3).

Long-term AFR November 2009	
Semiannual compounding	3.97%
Compounding periods 10 years X 2	20
Formula	$\$21{,}000 \times (1 + (3.97\%/2))^{20}$
Amount	$31,113
Less tax	-21,000
Interest	$10,113

This interest is shown as an additional tax on the income tax return, but may be deducted as a business expense for the dealer. For individuals, the amount is included at line 8 of 2019 Form 1040 Schedule 2, with the notation "Section 453(l)(3) interest." For corporations, the amount is included at 2019 Form 1120 Schedule J, line 9f.

Suspended passive activity losses and installment sales

Operating losses from "passive activities" may be limited to the amount of income from passive activities for a tax year and suspended until additional passive activity income is generated or until the entire passive activity is disposed. See Chapter 8.[46]

When the disposition of the entire interest is done using an installment sale, the suspended losses are allowed based on a ratio of the gain recognized for a tax year to the total gross profit from the sale.[47]

For example, Jane Taxpayer made an installment sale of her entire interest in a commercial building during 20X1. She had $500,000 of suspended passive activity losses for the building. Her gross profit for the sale was $1,000,000. $500,000 of the profit was taxable for 20X1.

Here are suspended passive activity losses she may deduct for 20X1.

Gross profit taxable for 20X1		$ 500,000
Divided by total gross profit		/ 1,000,000
Ratio of taxable gross profit to total		0.50
Times suspended passive activity losses	500,000	
Deduction allowed for passive activity losses for 20X1		$ 250,000

A corporate tax trap – the alternative minimum tax (repealed)

The corporate alternative minimum tax was repealed, effective for tax years beginning after December 31, 2017 by the Tax Cuts and Jobs Act of 2017. The following discussion relates to previous tax years.

---

46   IRC § 469.
47   IRC § 469(g)(3).

Regular "C" corporations may be subject to the alternative minimum tax. Small corporations that have average annual gross receipts of no more than $7,500,000 for the 3 taxable years before the current taxable year are exempt from the AMT. The first taxable year of a corporation is exempt, and a $5,000,000 average gross receipts test applies for the second and third years of existence.[48]

If the alternative minimum tax does apply, there is a tax trap for installment sales. Alternative minimum taxable income includes an adjustment for "adjusted current earnings" or ACE.[49] The adjustment is an addition of 75% of the excess of ACE over the alternative minimum taxable income before the ACE adjustment.[50]

Real estate investment trusts (REITs) and S corporations are not subject to the adjustment for ACE.[51]

When computing ACE, installment sale reporting isn't allowed.[52] Therefore, larger corporations may not receive the benefits of an installment sale that they otherwise might expect.

As the installment sale income is reported for the regular tax, negative ACE adjustments may be allowed to help recover minimum tax credits.[53]

Effective for tax years beginning after December 31, 2017, corporate minimum tax credits are refundable under the Tax Cuts and Jobs Act of 2017. The recovery of corporate minimum tax credits was accelerated by the Coronavirus Aid, Relief and Economic Security (CARES) Act (P.L. 116-136), enacted on March 27, 2020. See your tax advisor for details and for help possibly filing a claim for a refund.

Income with respect of a decedent

We currently have a federal estate tax. Under the Tax Cuts and Jobs Act of 2018, the exemption equivalent has temporarily been doubled from $5 million to $10 million, indexed for inflation after 2010, effective for tax years beginning after 2017 and expiring for tax years after 2025. The exemption equivalent for 2020 is $11,580,000. The federal estate tax rate that applies for transfers exceeding the exemption equivalent is 40%.

When the estate tax is attributable to an item that will be taxable income to the estate, trust or heirs of the decedent, a tax deduction is allowed to reduce the impact of double taxation.[54] Items that are subject to both income tax after death and estate tax are called "income with respect of a decedent" (IRD). One item of income with respect of a decedent is untaxed income for an installment sale.

48	IRC § 55(e).
49	IRC § 56(c)(1).
50	IRC § 56(g)(1).
51	Treasury Regulations § 1.56(g)-1(a)(4).
52	IRC § 56(g)(4)(D)(iv).
53	IRC § 56(g)(2).
54	IRC § 691.

There are also deductions that are allowable for both income tax reporting and estate tax reporting. A real estate-related item is property tax that was assessed before death but wasn't paid yet.

Deductions with respect of a decedent (DRD) are subtracted from income with respect of a decedent to arrive at a net income with respect of a decedent amount. The federal estate tax is computed on a "with" and "without" basis to determine the estate tax attributable to income with respect of a decedent. As the income is collected, the deduction for estate tax is determined based on the ratio of income received for the tax year to the total income with respect of a decedent.

A similar computation applies to generation-skipping taxes.

The tax deduction for estate tax attributable to capital gains is reported on the related part of Schedule D.[55] The tax deduction for other income is reported on Schedule A as a miscellaneous itemized deduction.

For example, Jane Taxpayer was deceased on December 31, 2019. She had a taxable estate (after the exemption) of $6,000,000. None of her beneficiaries were skip persons and generation-skipping tax did not apply to her estate. Her estate included an installment sale with $200,000 of untaxed income. She had no other income with respect of a decedent, but had deductions with respect of a decedent of $5,000 of property taxes unpaid at her death. Her estate had taxable installment sale income of $20,000 for 2020.

Taxable estate before IRD Adjustment		$6,000,000
IRD – installment sale	$200,000	
DRD – property taxes	-5,000	
Net IRD		-195,000
Taxable estate "without" IRD		$5,805,000
Estate tax with IRD		$2,400,000
Estate tax without IRD		2,322,000
Estate tax on IRD		$ 78,000
Installment sale income for 2020		$20,000
Divided by total IRD		/ 200,000
Fraction collected		0.10
Times Estate tax on IRD		X 78,000
Deduction for Estate Tax on IRD for 2020		$ 7,800

This deduction will be reported on Part II of Schedule D to offset the long-term capital gain from the installment sale.

55   IRC § 691(c)(4).

The Eighth Circuit Court of Appeals has ruled that income had to be reported for previously untaxed installment sale income when the note provided that all future payments would be cancelled on the death of the payee/buyer, who was related to the obligor/seller.[56]

"Cutting Edge" estate planning strategy – installment sale to a "defective" grantor trust

How can you "freeze" the estate and gift tax value of real estate that you expect to rapidly appreciate while keeping control of the asset and avoiding an income tax consequence from a sale to an estate planning trust?

An estate planning strategy that is currently popular is to take advantage of differences between the income tax rules and the estate tax rules that apply to trusts. A taxpayer can create a trust that is treated as owned by the taxpayer and so disregarded for income tax reporting, but is treated as not owned by the taxpayer for estate tax reporting. When such a trust is created intentionally, it is called an "intentionally defective grantor trust" or IDGT.

The trust is made defective by giving the creator or grantor of the trust (who is also the seller of the property) certain "prohibited" powers, such as the power to substitute assets of equal value in a nonfiduciary capacity or the power of a nonadverse party to add beneficiaries. (This is not a complete list.)

An installment sale to an IDGT can be used to "freeze" the value of the sold asset for estate and gift reporting, without an income tax consequence until the death of the seller. No gain or loss is reported by the selling taxpayer during his or her lifetime. You can't sell an asset to yourself for a taxable gain. No interest is reported for interest payments for the installment note. The grantor/seller reports any income earned from the property by the trust on his or her individual income tax return. Since the income tax is the obligation of the grantor/seller, there is no gift subject to federal gift tax for payment of the income tax by the grantor/seller.

Since the trust is respected for estate and gift tax reporting, transfers of assets to the trust are subject to gift tax.

The Internal Revenue Service and the 8th Circuit Court of Appeals have ruled any unreported income from an installment sale to a related person using a self-canceling installment note is taxable on the initial income tax return of the estate when the note is canceled at the seller's death.[57] If the installment sale is paid off before the seller's death, no gain will be taxable to the seller's estate.

Restating the mechanics of the strategy, cash for the down payment is contributed to an irrevocable trust that is "disregarded" for income tax reporting. This cash transfer is reported on a gift tax return as a taxable gift. An installment sale of real estate is made

---

56   *J.M. Frane,* 93-2 USTC ¶ 50,386.
57   Internal Revenue Code § 453B(f), Revenue Ruling 86-72, *R.E. Frane Estate,* 93-2 USTC ¶ 50,386 7/6/1993.

by the "seller/grantor" to the trust. The trust accumulates rental income minus operating expenses minus payments on the installment sale note. The only "income" the seller/grantor receives is the interest on the note. There is additional cash flow to the seller from the principal payments. The interest rate may be a low "applicable federal rate" to shift as much of the income from the property as possible to beneficiaries of the trust free of additional estate and gift tax. The seller/grantor reports the rental income and expenses from the property on his or her income tax return and pays the income taxes personally. The payment of income taxes is not subject to gift tax. No gain is reported for the sale of the property until the note is cancelled at death and the interest for the installment note is ignored as income and a deduction on the income tax return of the seller/grantor. If the note is paid off before the death of the seller, there will be no taxable income relating to the installment sale at the seller's death (and none during his or her lifetime).

This is only an introduction to this strategy as an item for your checklist of planning ideas for real estate. You should only implement this strategy under the guidance of qualified legal counsel.

Also consider that this strategy eliminates the basis adjustment for inherited property at death. With the increased exemption equivalents and even with the exemption equivalents that will remain after 2025 ($5 million per individual, indexed for inflation), this strategy will not produce the optimum tax result for all families.

Conclusion

Installment sales remain one of the most powerful tools in the tax planning arsenal for real estate. They are useful for stretching additional interest income from deferred taxes, managing cash flow by matching the payment of income taxes with cash collections, and for estate planning by "freezing" the value of the property sold in the seller's estate.

#

For more information on installment sales, see IRS Publication 537.

5
Tax-Deferred Section 1031 Real Estate Exchanges

The tax-deferred exchange (also called "tax free exchanges" and "1031 exchanges") remains the most important tool in planning for non-personal real estate transactions.

With the 3.8% federal surtax on net investment income, which became effective on January 1, 2013, and the increase in the federal income tax rate from 15% to 20% also effective January 1, 2013 for long-term capital gains for certain high-income taxpayers, tax-deferred exchanges will probably become even more popular.

A highly-publicized proposal for the Tax Cuts and Jobs Act of 2017 to repeal tax-deferred exchanges for real estate was NOT enacted. Tax-deferred exchanges for personal property, such as motor vehicles and business equipment, were repealed, effective for dispositions after December 31, 2017. (Exchanges of personal property initiated during 2017 can be completed, provided the other requirements are met.)

Also see Chapter 7 relating to depreciation. The liberalization of the expense election and bonus depreciation should result in an offsetting deduction for any income relating to a tax deferred exchange of personal property.

What can be exchanged?

There has been some discussion about curtailing the scope of real estate transactions qualifying for this treatment. For example, a motel would have to be exchanged for a motel; an apartment complex for an apartment complex.

So far, this has not developed. Any type of real estate held for productive use in a trade or business or for investment may be exchanged for any other type. A motel may be exchanged for a dairy pasture.

A little-known exception for depreciable real estate is commercial property acquired after 1980 and before 1987 for which accelerated depreciation was elected under the Accelerated Cost Recovery System. Since this property is Section 1245 recovery property, it is not like-kind with other depreciable real estate, which is Section 1250 recovery property.[58] If you have such an exchange, segregate amounts allocable to the exchange of the building from the amounts allocable to the exchange of the land. Most of the gain should be attributable to the land and should qualify for deferral. Exchanges of these properties are very rare, so you probably won't have to be concerned with this rule.

Personal residences and vacation homes do not qualify for tax-deferred exchanges.

---

58   IRC Section 1245(a)(5), before repeal by the Tax Reform Act of 1986.

Real estate that is "property held primarily for sale," such as a home built for sale, also does not qualify for tax-deferred exchange treatment.

The IRS has issued proposed reliance regulations updating the rules for Section 1031 tax deferred exchanges under the Tax Cuts and Jobs Act of 2017.[59]

Since the Tax Cuts and Jobs Act limits exchanges to real estate the IRS defines real estate for Section 1031 in the proposed regulations. "The term real property under section 1031 and §§ 1.1031(a)-1 through 1.1031(k)-1 means land and improvements to land, unsevered natural products of land, and water and air space superjacent to land. Under paragraph (a)(5) of this section, an interest in real property of a type described in this paragraph (a)(1), including fee ownership, co-ownership, a leasehold, an option to acquire real property, an easement, or a similar interest is real property for purposes of section 1031 and this section."[60]

The committee reports for the Tax Cuts and Jobs Act and the preamble for the proposed regulations state that real estate qualifying for Section 1031 tax-deferred exchange before the Act should still qualify after the Act.

Items attached to the property can be evaluated whether they are real property based on these factors.

(1) The manner in which the distinct asset is affixed to real property;

(2) Whether the distinct asset is designed to be removed or to remain in place;

(3) The damage that removal of the distinct asset would cause to the item itself or to the real property to which it is affixed;

(4) Any circumstances that suggest the expected period of affixation is not indefinite; and

(5) The time and expense required to move the distinct asset.[61]

Machinery generally isn't an inherently permanent structure that is real property. If the machinery serves the inherently permanent structure and does not produce or contribute to the production of income other than for the use or occupancy of space, it is real property.[62]

The proposed regulations include an example of partitions. Non-load-bearing drywall partitions that would have to be demolished to remove them are real property. Modular partitions that are designed to be moveable and can easily be removed when a tenant vacates the premises are not real property.[63]

---

59   REG-117589-18, June 12, 2020.
60   Proposed Treasury Regulations § 1.1031(a)-3(a)(1).
61   Proposed regulations § 1.1031(a)-3(a)(2)(ii)(C).
62   Proposed regulations § 1.1031(a)-3(a)(2)(ii)(D).
63   Proposed regulations § 1.1031(a)-3(b)(9).

The rules in the proposed regulations only control the status of property as real property for a Section 1031 tax deferred exchange. They do not determine the status of property for depreciation or depreciation recapture.[64]

I recommend that you and your tax advisor consult the proposed regulations to evaluate whether the components of your property are real estate qualifying for an exchange.

Exchanges for partnership interests do not qualify for tax-deferral. If the real estate interest received is converted or contributed to a partnership shortly after the exchange, the transaction may be "collapsed" and the deferral disallowed.

The gain will not be deferred for an exchange involving foreign real estate and U.S. real estate.

If an exchange is made with a "related party," any sale by the related party within two years after the exchange will result in the gain or loss being recognized on the date of the sale. This rule does not apply if the sale is made after the death of the related party or taxpayer within the two-year period.

Tenants in common interests or "TICs"

As I stated above, partnership interests don't qualify for tax-deferred exchanges, even when the sole asset of a partnership is real estate.

This has created a practical problem for many taxpayers. They might simply want to invest in a bigger project or might want to eliminate the management headaches of renting single family homes or duplexes.

An alternative to a partnership interest that can qualify for a tax-deferred exchange is an "undivided interest" or "tenant in common" interest in a piece of real estate. The shares of income and expenses, including fees of a professional management company, can be allocated to the various owners according to their ownership interests.

In some cases, the IRS has attacked tenant in common arrangements and said they were actually partnerships. In a sensitive tax situation such as a tax-free exchange, certainty of the outcome is essential. The IRS has issued safe harbor guidelines in Revenue Procedure 2002-22, 2002-1 CB 733 for organizers to secure an advance ruling from the IRS that the arrangement qualifies as a tenant in common interest. See a tax advisor for details, or you can look up the Revenue Procedure at the IRS web site, www.irs.gov.

Alternative trust arrangements

The tenancy-in-common structure has proven to be unwieldy. Taking actions, including selling the property, requires that the owners be unanimous.

---

64 Proposed regulations § 1.1031(a)-3(a)(6).

Alternative forms that the IRS has approved under certain circumstances include an Illinois land trust[65] and a Delaware statutory trust.[66] These arrangements were deemed to be the same as personally holding title to the property. The IRS stressed that the trustees had very limited powers. In Revenue Ruling 78-371, the trustee had sufficient powers that the trust was considered an association taxable as a corporation.

Proceed with caution, including getting good legal counsel.

A typical estate planning trust or revocable living trust is a disregarded entity for income tax reporting purposes during the lifetime of the grantors, so the fact that real estate is held in one of these trusts has no significance relating to a Section 1031 exchange.

Is an election required?

The tax-deferred exchange section is not elective. If you have an exchange of like-kind property, it automatically applies.

What about losses?

Not only gain, but loss may be deferred from an exchange, even when "boot" is received. Therefore, a transaction that will result in a loss should not be structured as an exchange but an outright sale.

When must a gain be recognized?

When cash or property other than real estate is received as part of an exchange transaction, those are unlike assets, called "boot." The lesser of the net boot received or the potential gain is recognized as taxable gain. When personal property is received or sold, it should be separately valued (hopefully in the contract) so this computation is made consistently between the buyer and seller.

If a Section 179 expense election has been made for real property, such as Qualified Improvement property, that property for which the Section 179 basis adjustment applies is Section 1245 property, subject to depreciation recapture. It appears to me that property is not like-kind to Section 1250 real estate or land received in an exchange.[67]

Note that items clearing through escrow, such as the settlement of rent deposits and the payment of property taxes, may represent "cash received" or "cash paid." For example, if property taxes of $10,000 are paid through escrow, this represents "cash received" applied to property taxes. (The property tax expense will be a deduction that could offset recognized taxable gain.)

The debt relieved for the property sold is compared to the debt incurred for the property received. Any excess of debt relieved over debt incurred is "boot."

---

65 Revenue Ruling 92-105.
66 Revenue Ruling 2004-86.
67 Internal Revenue Code § 1245(a)(3)(C).

For example:

John Taxpayer exchanged Blackacre for Whiteacre. His tax basis in Blackacre was $500,000. Whiteacre has a fair market value of $1,000,000. Blackacre was subject to a mortgage of $200,000. Whiteacre is subject to a mortgage of $100,000. John also received net cash of $50,000 for the transaction.

<u>Gain realized</u>

Received:		
Whiteacre	$1,000,000	
Debt relieved	200,000	
Cash	<u>50,000</u>	
Total		$1,250,000
Exchanged:		
Tax Basis Blackacre	500,000	
Debt acquired	<u>100,000</u>	
Total		<u>600,000</u>
Gain realized		<u>$ 650,000</u>
<u>Boot received:</u>		
Debt relieved	$ 200,000	
Debt acquired	<u>100,000</u>	
Net debt relieved		$ 100,000
Net cash received		<u>50,000</u>
Net boot received		<u>$ 150,000</u>
Gain recognized (lesser of realized gain or boot)		<u>$ 150,000</u>
Tax basis of Whiteacre		
Fair market value		$1,000,000
Gain realized	$ 650,000	
Less gain recognized	<u>150,000</u>	
Deferred gain		<u>500,000</u>
Tax basis		<u>$ 500,000</u>

Special rule for Section 1250 property

See Chapter 2, Other Sales of Real Estate

When depreciable real estate is depreciated using an accelerated method, including using MACRS for land improvements and bonus depreciation for Qualified Improvement Property (see Chapter 7), the excess of depreciation claimed over straight-line depreciation is recaptured as ordinary income when the property is sold.

This ordinary income is deferred in a Section 1031 tax-deferred exchange, provided the value of Section 1250 real estate (depreciable real estate) received is equal to or greater than the value of Section 1250 real estate surrendered.

If the value of the Section 1250 real estate received is less than the value of the Section 1250 real estate surrendered, ordinary income is currently taxable for the GREATER of:

(1) The amount of gain otherwise recognized as a result of the transaction (for boot or non-like-kind property received), or

(2) The depreciation that would have been recaptured under Internal Revenue Code Section 1250 if the disposition was a cash sale, less the fair market value of Section 1250 property received in the exchange.[68]

Since more real estate now is Qualified Improvement Property for which bonus depreciation will be claimed, this provision will apply to more Section 1031 exchanges.

Allocating basis for acquired properties

When properties are exchanged, the taxpayer should get an appraisal of the property received allocating the purchase price between land, building, and property improvements, such as driveways and swimming pools, in order to construct the depreciation schedule for the property.

See the section on cost segregation and like-kind exchanges below and Chapter 7.

Non-simultaneous exchanges

Thanks to the *Starker* decision, Congress and the IRS have defined certain situations where an exchange may be made on a non-simultaneous basis.[69]

In order to qualify for a non-simultaneous (deferred) exchange, replacement property must be identified within 45 days after the transfer of the relinquished property (identification period) and the replacement property must be received within the earlier of 180 days after the transfer of the relinquished property or the due date, including extensions, of the seller's income tax returns (exchange period). If the sale is made close to the end of the year, the seller will usually need to extend the due date of his or her income tax returns.

As COVID-19 relief, the IRS has clarified on its website that the deadlines for the 45-day identification period and the 180-day completion period that would have fallen during the period from April 1, 2020 and before July 15, 2020 was extended to July 15, 2020.[70]

In structuring these transactions, the net proceeds from the "sale" leg of the transaction are deposited with an intermediary called a "qualified intermediary" or "QI." In other words, the seller may not have control of the funds during the intervening period. A

68　　Internal Revenue Code § 1250(d)(4).
69　　Treasury Regulations § 1.1031(k)-1.
70　　See also Notice 2020-23, extending the due date for certain administrative acts.

person who has had an agency relationship with the person making the exchange during the two-year period ending on the date of transfer of the first of the relinquished properties can't be a qualified intermediary for the transaction. Disqualified agency relationships include acting as that person's employee, attorney, accountant, investment banker or broker, or real estate agent or broker.[71]

The proposed regulations (REG-117589-18) cover the issue that a taxpayer would be considered in constructive receipt of all of the exchange funds held by a qualified intermediary if the taxpayer is able to direct the qualified intermediary to use the funds to acquire property that is not of a like kind to the taxpayer's relinquished property. The proposed regulations state that personal property that is incidental to real property acquired in an exchange will not disqualify the transaction.

Personal property is incidental to real property acquired in an exchange if (A) In standard commercial transactions, the personal property is typically transferred together with the real property; and (B) The aggregate fair market value of the incidental personal property transferred with the real property does not exceed 15 percent of the aggregate fair market value of the replacement real property.[72]

When evaluating the replacement property, avoid exceeding the 15 percent limit by using funds other than those held by the QI to pay for excess incidental personal property.

Remember the incidental personal property is "boot" (unlike property received), resulting in some taxable income for the exchange.[73]

Be careful when selecting an intermediary. One of my clients had his exchange funds embezzled!

During May 2007, one of the largest qualified intermediaries in the country, 1031 Tax Group, LLC of Richmond, Virginia filed for bankruptcy. The company was holding millions of dollars for clients who weren't able to complete their exchanges. The company listed about $160 million of debts owed creditors.

Another big qualified intermediary, Southwest Exchange, was also forced into liquidation during 2007 owing customers about $100 million.

When the exchange can't be completed within the 180-day period, the seller who has deposited funds with the qualified intermediary must report the sale as paid at the expiration of that period. The sale is usually reported as an installment sale. (See the section on installment sale reporting for like-kind exchanges, below.)

---

71   Treasury Regulations § 1.1031(k)-1(k).
72   Proposed Treasury Regulations § 1.1031(k)-1(g)(7)(iii).
73   Proposed Treasury Regulations § 1.1031(k)-1(g)(8)(vi).

The seller might be able to claim an offsetting loss for any funds that can't be recovered. When the transaction relates to a sale of business or rental property, the loss should be an "above the line" deduction. The loss might not be deductible in the same year that the gain from the failed exchange has to be reported. In order to deduct the loss, you have to be able to determine an amount that can't be recovered under an "all events test." If the qualified intermediary has filed for reorganization under Bankruptcy Code Chapter 13, you might not be able to establish the amount of the loss until a plan of reorganization is completed.

If you find yourself in this situation, get help from a qualified tax advisor.

The most important thing you can do to protect yourself is to *know your qualified intermediary*. You could request a bond, but this requirement will disqualify all but the largest QIs. Another approach is to arrange a letter of credit. A friend of mine who was a qualified intermediary set up a two-signature requirement to make payments from the account where the funds are deposited. The second signature is from a person who is independent from the person making the exchange.

In order to qualify for a non-simultaneous exchange, the replacement properties must be identified in writing by the taxpayer and hand delivered, mailed, telecopied, or otherwise sent before the end of the identification period. This step should be carefully documented. There are various persons who could be notified, but the best choice is the intermediary. Replacement real estate should be clearly described by a legal description, street address, or distinguishable name.

The taxpayer may identify more than one replacement property. There can be any number of relinquished properties for a deferred exchange. For the replacement properties, the choices are (a) up to three properties without regard to the fair market values of the properties (three property rule) or (b) any number of properties provided the aggregate fair market value at the end of the identification period doesn't exceed 200% of the aggregate fair market value of all the relinquished properties as of the date they were transferred by the taxpayer (200% rule).[74]

From a practical standpoint, almost everyone follows the three-property rule, because it's much easier to implement.

If too many properties are identified at the end of the identification period, then the taxpayer is treated as if no replacement property had been identified. There are two exceptions to this rule: (1) Replacement property received before the end of the identification period "counts"; (2) Replacement property identified before the end of the identification period and received before the end of the exchange period, provided 95% of the aggregate fair market value of all identified properties are received (95% rule).

The replacement property must be received no later than the earlier of (a) 180 days after the date on which the taxpayer transfers the property relinquished in the exchange, or

---

74 Treasury Regulations § 1.1031(k)-1(c)(4).

(b) the due date (including extensions) for the transferor's tax return for the taxable year when the property was relinquished. (You should usually extend the due date of the tax return for the year of the exchange when the sale happens late in the year.)

For example: John Taxpayer has a non-simultaneous exchange of Blackacre on December 31, 20X2. He must designate a replacement property in writing no later than February 14, 20X3. The purchase of the replacement property must be completed no later than June 29, 20X3, provided John filed for an extension. If he did not, the purchase of the replacement property must be completed no later than April 15, 20X3.

These deferred exchanges can be very suspenseful. It seems Murphy's Law reigns – if anything can go wrong, it will. 45 days is a very short window for identifying replacement property, so it's better to identify it before the sale "leg" closes. The seller of the replacement property has a very effective negotiation "hammer" against the buyer, who might have to pay a big tax bill if the purchase "leg" falls through.

What if the exchange "falls apart" and isn't completed? If the cash isn't distributed until the year after the year of sale, the sale can be reported using the installment method. (See Chapter 4 and the section on installment sale reporting for like-kind exchanges below.) The reason is the amounts held by the qualified intermediary are not considered to have been received by the seller. The qualified intermediary is required to distribute the funds after the 180-day "exchange period." Remember that the sale proceeds applied to pay off the debt on the sold property will be considered received when the sale closed. Therefore, part of the gain may be taxable for the year of the sale and the balance in the year the replacement period expires.

Reverse exchanges

Exchanges can be structured so the replacement property is acquired before relinquished property is sold. The taxpayer loans funds or guarantees a loan to the intermediary who then purchases the replacement property to hold and uses the proceeds from the relinquished property to pay off the loan. The relinquished property must be sold and the exchange closed within 180 days after the replacement property is purchased. The IRS has issued safe-harbor guidelines for reverse exchanges in Revenue Procedure 2000-37.

Reverse exchanges are sensitive transactions that should only be done under the guidance of qualified tax advisors. Putting together the financing is very complex.

Sale of a principal residence acquired as part of a tax-deferred exchange

The tax law was changed effective for sales or exchanges after October 22, 2004 so that a principal residence acquired in a tax-deferred exchange won't qualify for the exclusion for the sale of a principal residence unless the property has been held more than five years. This situation could happen when a taxpayer exchanges rental real estate for another home that is rented for a period of time, but is later converted from a rental home to a principal residence. A side effect of this rule is the principal residence evidently won't qualify for a partial exclusion if the residence is sold early due to a hardship or unforeseen circumstances.

Installment sale reporting for like-kind exchanges

When you have taxable income because there is "boot" received for a like-kind exchange and part of the boot is a note payable to the seller, you are eligible for installment sale reporting for the taxable income. See Chapter 4 on installment sales.

If a non-simultaneous exchange doesn't work out and the sale proceeds are received after the year of sale, the gain may be reported as an installment sale. Since the "payment" applied to pay off the debt on the property is received on the closing date, the gain attributable to that payment is taxable (on the installment sale form) in the year of the sale. Cash held by the intermediary is taxable when the 180 day period for completing the installment sale is over, even if the funds aren't received from the intermediary.

Some intermediaries have failed to distribute funds for the purchase of properties or to sellers for failed exchanges. They have gone bankrupt or had funds embezzled. Be careful who you are doing business with. The seller could be stuck with a loss for a non-business bad debt (capital loss) or a theft loss that may not match with the income reported for the installment sale – not a happy situation.

Cost segregation and like-kind exchanges

One of the hottest services for the real estate industry is cost segregation studies. See Chapter 7.

The purpose of a cost segregation study is to break down the purchase price or tax basis of real estate to get faster depreciation. The depreciable life for a commercial building is 39 years and for a residential building is 27.5 years. The depreciable life for land improvements is 15 years and for some electrical wiring associated with computer equipment is 5 years.

Since the Tax Cuts and Jobs Act of 2017 repealed Section 1031 exchanges for property other than real estate in tax years after 2017 and items for which a Section 179 expense election was made are reclassified to Section 1245 property apparently not eligible for a tax-deferred exchange with other Section 1250 depreciable real estate or land, it may be necessary to get cost segregation studies to properly report a Section 1031 tax deferred exchange.

A side effect of cost segregation is to make like-kind exchanges more complex and harder to qualify. It's easier to make an exchange of a building that is simply being depreciated as such.

See the discussion relating to proposed regulations relating to the classification of property as real property qualifying for a Section 1031 tax deferred exchange. (REG-117589-18.) The proposed regulations state that land improvements that qualify for accelerated depreciation also qualify as real estate for a Section 1031 tax deferred exchange.

Cost segregation studies are designed to identify items that might not be real estate and might qualify for depreciation using shorter MACRS lives.

The longer term you expect to keep the real estate, the more favorable a cost-segregation study is. If you expect to exchange the property in a fairly short time (guess less than eleven years), you are probably better off not going through the cost segregation exercise.

Related party exchanges

If a taxpayer has a tax-deferred exchange property with a related person and within two years of the last transfer of the exchange, the related person disposes of the property relinquished or the taxpayer disposes of the property received, the previously untaxed gain will become taxable for the year of disposition.[75]

Related persons include (1) corporations, S corporations and partnerships that are controlled, directly or indirectly by the seller; (2) a seller and a trust with the seller or his or her spouse as a beneficiary; and (3) a selling estate and a beneficiary of the estate, unless the sale is in satisfaction of a pecuniary bequest.

There are three exceptions to this income acceleration rule: (1) a disposition after the death of either person; (2) a disposition in a compulsory or involuntary conversion, or a threat of one; (3) if the IRS is satisfied the exchange didn't have as one of its principal purposes the avoidance of federal income tax.

For the last exception, the taxpayer will have to apply for a ruling from the IRS. In evaluating whether income tax avoidance applies, the IRS is mostly looking for "basis shifting." The IRS surprised the tax consulting community with surprisingly liberal rulings, approving two sales by related parties within the two-year period on the same day.[76]

The two-year period is extended when (a) there is an option to purchase the property; (b) another person has a right to purchase the property (contract of sale); or (c) there is a short sale arrangement for the property (contract for a future sale).

Like-kind exchanges of foreign and U.S. property

Real estate held in the United States is not like kind to real estate held outside the United States.[77]

---

75   IRC § 1031(f).
76   Letter Rulings 200820017 and 200820025, both issued February 7, 2008.
77   IRC § 1031(h).

Vacation rental homes

The general rule for vacation homes that are used by a taxpayer as a second home for vacations is these are personal use assets that don't qualify for inclusion in a tax-free exchange, even though investment may be a significant purpose of holding the property.[78]

The IRS issued guidelines permitting vacation homes that are principally rented to unrelated persons to qualify for tax-free exchanges. In order to qualify for the relinquished property, (a) the home must have been owned by the taxpayer for at least 24 months before the exchange; (b) for the two 12-month periods immediately before the exchange (i) the taxpayer must have rented the home to another person or persons at a fair rental for at least 14 days or more, and (ii) the period of the taxpayer's personal use of the home may not exceed the greater of 14 days or 10% of the number of days during the 12-month period that the home is rented at a fair rental rate.[79]

For the replacement property, the home must be owned by the taxpayer for at least 24 months immediately after the exchange. During the 24 months immediately after the exchange, the taxpayer must meet the same use requirements as for the relinquished property, above.

If a taxpayer believes the replacement property will meet the use requirements when preparing the tax return for the year of exchange, he or she should report it as an exchange on the original return. If the property later fails the use tests, the tax return for the year of exchange should be amended to eliminate the tax-free exchange treatment and report the taxable income for the exchange.

The procedure for vacation home rental homes is effective for exchanges on or after March 10, 2008.

Reporting like-kind exchanges

The IRS form for reporting like-kind exchanges is Form 8824. You can get a copy at the IRS web site, www.irs.gov.

California enacted AB 92 on June 17, 2013. Under this new law, taxpayers who complete a Section 1031 exchange of California property for out of state property after 2013 are required to file an annual information return with the California Franchise Tax Board until the replacement property is sold and the gain is recognized. (If the replacement property is exchanged, presumably you would continue to file the information report.) The information is reported using Form 3840. If the report isn't made, the Franchise Tax Board can compute what the tax would be if the deferred California gain was recognized and send a bill to the taxpayer.

---

78   *Moore v. Commissioner*, T.C. Memo. 2007-134, May 30, 2007.
79   Revenue Procedure 2008-16, 2008-10 I.R.B. 547.

The Franchise Tax Board has allowed some taxpayers to "clean up" reporting that was accidentally missed. Don't plan on relying on their generosity, be sure to comply with the reporting requirements.

This explanation isn't complete. Be sure to check the reporting requirements for all of the states in which properties involved in an exchange are located. This is another good reason to hire tax professionals for planning and reporting these transactions.

Conclusion - Get Help!

This is a simplified explanation of some of the issues relating to tax-deferred exchanges. These are sensitive transactions, usually with high-stakes results. We highly recommend that you get professional help beyond the real estate agent to put a deal together. An investment in fees for legal and tax consulting help can pay off in avoiding unpleasant surprises later.

#

For more information about like-kind exchanges, see IRS Publication 544, Sales and Other Dispositions of Assets, starting at page 11. You can get a copy at www.irs.gov.

6
What are the different forms available for real estate operations?

There are many ways that real estate operations can be conducted. The ability to shield the investor's other investments from potential liabilities, including personal injury lawsuits, are as important as the tax considerations for structuring operations. Remember that insurance, including umbrella policies, can also be secured for liability protection.

Many different tax law changes were enacted as part of the Tax Cuts and Jobs Act of 2017. These changes could have a significant impact when choosing the form for operating a business. The changes relating to "C" corporations are mostly "permanent" (until Congress changes them again) and effective for tax years beginning after December 31, 2017. The changes relating to non-corporate entities (including S corporations) are mostly effective for tax years beginning after December 31, 2017 and expire after tax years beginning in 2025.

Decisions for the form of operating a business have long-term consequences. Since the Tax Cuts and Jobs Act of 2017 was enacted by excluding Democrat representatives in Congress, many of the tax cuts could be reversed if the Democrats get control of Congress and the White House.

We are discussing areas with legal considerations and I remind you that I am not a lawyer. Although there are services available to form corporations and limited liability companies (LLCs) for a small investment, I believe it's worthwhile to make the investment in legal fees. You might want to incorporate or form an LLC in a different state (such as Delaware) for important legal reasons.

I am mostly focusing on federal tax considerations here. State tax considerations are also important and should be investigated. Many states don't conform with federal tax laws, and the state laws are also inconsistent.

Also, I'm not going to get into too much detail about title issues here, because you should be getting legal advice about that area. There are important estate and marital planning implications to be considered.

This chapter is just going to be a thumbnail explanation of choice of entity alternatives. You really should consult with a lawyer and a qualified tax advisor about your situation.

Sole ownership

A person can have sole ownership in real estate.

This is the simplest form of ownership.

If the real estate is a rental property, the income and deductions will be reported on Schedule E on the owner's individual income tax return.

You can get a copy of Form 1040, Schedule E and instructions at the IRS web site, www.irs.gov.

The owner may be liable for personal injury claims, should a personal injury take place on the property.

The owner might qualify for the federal tax deduction for business income not taxed to a C corporation.

Joint tenancy

When individuals own property as joint tenants, they literally own it "together." All of the joint tenants are subject to personal injury claims for the property.

For income tax purposes, you divide the income and deductions by the number of joint tenants to determine the amounts to report on each owner's income tax returns.

When one of the joint tenants dies, that interest "disappears" and is divided up equally among the surviving joint tenants. The decedent's joint tenancy share is reported on his or her estate tax return. The decedent can't direct in a will or trust who will inherit the joint tenancy interest.

Only the decedent's share is eligible for a basis adjustment at death.

When a husband and wife buy a home, the "default" title set up by many title companies is as joint tenants. From an estate planning point of view, this may not be the best choice. Consult with an estate planning attorney about the laws in your state about this matter.

A disadvantage of joint tenancy property is that a co-owner has a right to partition or break the joint tenancy to gain control over who can inherit it or to give it away.

The noncorporate owners might qualify for the federal tax deduction for business income not taxed to a C corporation. The income of a C corporation would be taxed at corporate income tax rates.

Tenants in common or undivided interests

Tenants in common or undivided interests are a way for many individuals to have ownership in real estate in varying shares. For example, John Smith might own a 10% undivided interest and his sister, Jane, might have a 20% interest.

The income and deductions for the property are generally allocated in proportion to the ownership interests.

You can also "mix and match" other forms of ownership with undivided interests. For example, John, Jill and Fred might own a 10% undivided interest as joint tenants. Ted and Alice might own a 20% interest as community property.

Generally, the owner of an undivided interest has the right to direct who will inherit it in his or her will or trust. (An exception is when the undivided interest is owned by joint tenants.)

The tenants in common have joint and several liability for personal injury claims, so each of them can be held 100% liable by the plaintiff. If a co-owner pays a disproportionate share of a liability, he or she may seek a contribution from the others. (Again, please discuss liability issues with your legal counsel.)

Also, see the discussion about tenants in common, or "TICs" in Chapter 5.

The noncorporate owners might qualify for the federal tax deduction for business income not taxed to a C corporation. The income of a C corporation would be taxed at corporate income tax rates.

Community property

Community property is a way for married persons to own property. Not all states are "community property states." Since community property evolved from Roman law, the community property states were mostly formerly Spanish and French territories. How community property operates is different in each state, so you should consult with a local attorney to determine your rights and responsibilities as a community property owner.

The community property states are Arizona, California, Idaho, Louisiana, Nevada, New Mexico, Texas, Washington and Wisconsin.

With the Supreme Court's *Windsor* decision in 2013, it's now clear the federal government recognizes marital rights of same-sex married couples who are legally married in a jurisdiction that permits such marriages, including the right as a resident of a community property state to hold title as community property.

The tax consequences of community property owned by same sex registered domestic partners is uncertain and there are also federal tax questions relating to community property of heterosexual registered domestic partners, usually individuals who are over age 62. Discuss this issue with your legal and tax advisors. It's tragic that laws intended to help people in certain circumstances can become tax traps.

As I understand it, in California (my home state), property acquired through the joint efforts of a married couple during their marriage is community property. Property received by an individual by gift or inheritance is not community property. Property held as joint tenants by married partners is not community property for estate tax and related tax basis adjustment purposes of inherited property (discussed below), but is community property for other purposes. Married couples can divide community property into separate shares or transmute separate shares into community property. A partner may not gift or use marital property for a separate purpose without the consent of the other partner. Income from separate property is separate property. Income from community property is community property. (Confused enough?)

Again, as I understand it, in California a deceased partner may direct in a will or trust who will inherit his or her share of the community property. If the deceased partner doesn't make such a direction or dies without a will or trust (intestate), the surviving partner automatically inherits the decedent's share of the community property. (Think any wills or trusts might get "lost" because of this?)

There is another form of title in California, Community Property With Rights of Survivorship. The direction that the surviving partner will receive the property after the death of a decedent partner is included in the form of title, superseding an extraneous will or trust.

Most married couples file joint income tax returns, so all of the income and deductions with respect to real estate held as community property is reported on the joint return. For those who elect to file separately, one-half of the income and deductions with respect to community property should be reported on the income tax return for each partner.

Community property has a tax advantage that, on the death of the first spouse to die, the entire basis of the property is adjusted to the fair market value on the date of death.[80] (The tax consequences for community property owned by registered domestic partners is uncertain.) We call this a "double step-up" in basis, but it can be a "double step-down" if the value has actually declined after the property was acquired. This adjustment is a fresh start. The depreciation history is erased by the death of a married partner.

You can get a copy of IRS Publication 555, Community Property and IRS Publication 551, Basis of Assets at the IRS web site, www.irs.gov.

Noncorporate owners might qualify for the federal tax deduction for business income not taxed to a C corporation

---

80   IRC § 1014(b)(6).

Estate planning trusts

Revocable living trusts have become very popular as a method of avoiding the delays and formalities of probate. I view these trusts as a substitute for a will. The main advantages of revocable living trusts are privacy and speed of administration.

In order to get the benefits of a revocable living trust, you have to actually transfer assets to the trust. For real estate, this means changing the title of the property to the trust. There are many revocable living trusts that have been created but the property had to be processed though probate anyway, because it was never transferred to the trust. In California, a "Heggstad petition" can be filed to claim the decedent intended for property to be administered under the trust. This should be viewed as "cleanup" when property hasn't been titled properly.

During the lifetime of the creators, also called "grantors" of the trust, there is no tax effect. The trust is a substitute for a will, so the real impact doesn't happen until after a death.

There is an exception to be aware of. Congress has enacted a Centralized Partnership Audit Regime (CPAR), effective for partnership tax years beginning after 2017. The audit rules and rules for correcting errors on a partnership income tax return are more complex and can result in income taxation of adjustments at the maximum income tax rate for the type of partner. Partnerships with only qualifying partners may elect out of CPAR if the partnership has 100 or fewer partners. Trusts are NOT qualifying partners and grantor trusts are NOT disregarded under these rules. (An estate of a deceased partner IS a qualified partner.) You should discuss this issue with your estate planning attorney and your tax advisor.[81]

After a death, there is typically a division of the property into separate trusts. Depending on the terms of the trust and the Probate Code for the particular state that applies of the trust, the trustee may have the authority to make non-pro rata allocations of assets "in kind." Most tax practitioners believe that when such an allocation is made with this authority based on fair market values at the date of allocation, there is no resulting taxable gain or loss.[82] The allocation of assets is an important part of tax planning after a death, and should be done under the guidance of a qualified attorney.

As part of the estate planning process, the estate planning attorney should assure that the trustee has the discretion/authority to allocate shares in cash or in kind. It will make the administration process after a death much easier.

If the trustee doesn't have the authority to make "in kind" allocations, the allocation of assets on a non-pro rata basis is a taxable event.[83]

81	Treasury Regulations § 301.6221(b)(1).
82	Revenue Ruling 69-486.
83	Revenue Ruling 69-486.

If the revocable trust was for a married couple, one of the trusts will be a survivor's revocable trust for the survivor's share of the assets.

A second trust, sometimes called a "credit trust" or "bypass trust" is created to use the lifetime exemption equivalent of the decedent.

The estate and gift tax exemption has been doubled from $5 million to $10 million, indexed for inflation after 2010, effective for tax years beginning after 2017 and expiring for tax years after 2025, at which time it will revert to about 1/2 the exemption for 2025. The exemption equivalent for 2020 is $11,580,000. Under the current federal estate tax laws, the estate tax exemption is "portable" for surviving spouses. This means the unused exemption for the last-deceased spouse (the last spouse the surviving spouse was married to and died before the surviving spouse's death) can be available for the surviving spouse, enabling a married couple to have a combined taxable estate of up to $23,160,000 and not be subject to estate tax.

The exemption increase expires after 2025. The IRS has issued guidance about what happens after 2025 to exemptions increased using portability elections made by estates of decedents who died before 2026. The exemption for the deceased spouse is not reduced and will be available for the surviving spouse if the surviving spouse qualifies (does not remarry).[84]

A third trust, sometimes called a QTIP trust or a marital trust, is created to qualify for the marital exemption. Under the terms of the trust, the decedent directs who will ultimately receive the assets of the trust after the death of the surviving spouse. The assets of the trust are included in the taxable estate of the surviving spouse.

There are also adjustments with the various trusts for the generation-skipping tax, which I am not going to discuss in detail.

The point is, after a death, the situation becomes much more complex and expensive.

With the tax law changes in the Tax Cuts and Jobs Act of 2017, all Americans should review their estate plans. It could be a bypass trust is no longer desirable. Families should also evaluate whether existing bypass trusts should be distributed. You should only take these steps under the guidance of a qualified tax advisor and qualified legal counsel who are familiar with these new rules.

Also note that the various trusts that I've described can also be created under a will. Trusts created under a will are called testamentary trusts.

The trusts can have various provisions about the distribution of income. The trust may require that income be distributed currently, called a "simple trust." The trust may also give the trustee discretion about how much income will be distributed, called a "complex trust."

---

84 Treasury Regulations § 20.2010-1(c).

Income of a simple trust is taxable to the beneficiaries of the trust. ("Principal" items, such as capital gains, are usually taxed to the trust.)

Any income of a complex trust that is distributed to the beneficiaries is taxable to the beneficiaries. Any undistributed income plus principal items are taxed to the trust.

If the expenses of the trust exceed the income, then the items are not distributed to the beneficiaries, except on a final income tax return for the trust. There is a special rule for depreciation where it can "follow" the income distributed to the beneficiaries.

The shares of income and expenses that are to be reported by the beneficiaries for a taxable year are reported to them on Form 1041, Schedule K-1. The beneficiaries' shares of the income and deductions for the trust's real estate operations are reported on Form 1040, Schedule E, Part III.

Maximum federal income tax rates for trusts are reached at a very low taxable income threshold. Effective for the tax year beginning after December 31, 2019, the 37% maximum tax federal income tax rate applies to ordinary income (such as net rental income and interest income) when taxable income exceeds $12,950, indexed for inflation thereafter. The federal tax rate for long-term capital gains is 20% when taxable income exceeds the same threshold. The 3.8% surtax on net investment income also applies when taxable income exceeds the same threshold. (See chapter 14.) These tax increases will motivate taxpayers to reexamine their estate plans and whether existing trusts should be terminated.

When bypass trusts and marital trusts become irrevocable after the death of the grantor, they can have some asset protection characteristics by including "spendthrift clauses" and because of the separate nature of these trusts.

Trusts are noncorporate owners that might qualify for the federal tax deduction for business income not taxed to a C corporation.

You can get the following items at the IRS web site: Form 1041 and instructions; Publication 559, Survivors, Executors and Administrators; and Publication 448, Federal Estate and Gift Taxes.

"Title" trusts

Some real estate is held under a trust title for privacy. It's sort of an informal fictitious name. For example, the title might be "2091 First Street Trust." The purpose is to get some asset protection by making it more difficult for creditors to identify who owns a parcel of real estate.

For income tax reporting, these trusts are "grantor trusts" or a type of revocable living trust and the income and deductions are reported on the grantor/owner's individual income tax returns.

This technique is just a smokescreen. The assets are still subject to the general creditors of the grantor.

General partnerships

By joining their capital and talents together and sharing risks, individuals can take on much bigger projects than they could handle alone.

When a property requires active management, then some sort of business entity is required to operate it. When people join together, the simplest form of business entity is a general partnership.

General partnerships don't pay income taxes. They are a "pass through" entity. Each partner's share of the income, deductions and credits relating to the partnership activity for a tax year is reported on a Schedule K-1 form. Real estate activities from a partnership are usually reported on Form 1040, Schedule E, Part II.

A disadvantage of a general partnership is that the partners have joint and several liability for its obligations, including personal injury lawsuits.

In some cases, the partnership may generate taxable income that is passed through to the partners and taxed on their individual income tax returns, but may not be able to distribute cash because it is needed for investment in the partnership.

Partners don't qualify for some tax-advantaged benefits, like disability insurance and group-term life insurance.

Determining contributions to retirement plans relating to partnership income, including 401(k) plans, can be complicated and expensive. (Rental income isn't earned income, so it doesn't qualify for determining retirement plan contributions anyway.)

There are also many advantages of general partnerships.

1. Liabilities of the partnership "flow through" to the partners, creating "investment" and enabling the partners to claim tax deductions without having to pay cash currently.

2. There are many ways to structure compensation, including partner salaries, preferential or guaranteed returns based on capital investment, and others.

3. Salaries can be paid to general partners of real estate operations on which qualified retirement plan contributions can be based.

4. There can be special allocations of certain items, provided those allocations have "substantial economic effect."

5. Although not recommended, the partnership agreement can be informal and unwritten. This can be convenient when initially starting a venture, but lays the groundwork for disputes later. (A blessing and a curse.)

6. Elections are available to make "inside" basis adjustments for "outside" events, such as a partner's sale of his or her share or an inheritance of a partnership interest.

7. Liquidating distributions can be made to a retiring partner on a tax-deductible basis.

8. Partnership losses are passed through to the partners. This is helpful when the partnership is in a "start-up" mode.

9. It's easier for general partners to qualify as "active" under the passive activity loss rules, and thus currently deduct losses from the venture against other income.

10. U.S. residents and non-residents can participate.

11. Partnerships can be used for family income and estate planning purposes to transfer future appreciation to family members and allocate income from passive assets to lower-income family members. Partnership interests transferred as lifetime gifts can qualify for valuation discounts.

12. The liquidation rules are generally more favorable for partnerships than for corporations. This makes it easier to contribute property and later take it out. Remember, "the devil is in the details." For example, liquidations involving ordinary income items, such as uncollected accounts receivable of cash basis partnerships, substantially appreciated inventory (like a real estate housing development in process), and depreciation recapture, can result in accelerating ordinary income recognition to the year of liquidation.[85] Get professional tax planning advice for any major transaction.

The noncorporate owners might qualify for the federal tax deduction for business income not taxed to a C corporation. The income of a C corporation would be taxed at corporate income tax rates.

You can get Form 1065 and instructions; Publication 541, Partnerships, and Publication 1653, US Partnership Return of Income at the IRS web site, www.irs.gov.

Limited partnerships

Investors wanted to get the benefits of partnership ownership but also wanted to avoid the unlimited "joint and several" liability disadvantage. They also wanted to be able to have professional management and avoid investor involvement in the day-to-day operations of partnership operations.

---

85 IRC § 751.

The states enacted limited partnership laws. The limited partners typically only risk the amount they have invested in the partnership.

As a result, limited partners do not receive a tax "investment" for partnership general liabilities and are limited to the amount they invest plus any undistributed partnership income for deducting partnership losses.

There is an exception for "qualified nonrecourse indebtedness."[86] Qualified nonrecourse financing is financing provided by organizations in the business of lending for which no one is personally liable and secured by real estate used in the activity. The organizations include banks, savings and loan associations, credit unions, insurance companies, pension trusts, and government agencies. Loans guaranteed by federal, state or local government agencies also qualify.

The theory is, since no one is personally liable, all partners are allowed to participate.

Limited partnerships require formal partnership agreements and are registered with the states where they are doing business.

Limited partnerships also are required to have a general partner. Liability exposure can be minimized by having a corporation or a limited liability company as the general partner.

Like general partnerships, limited partnerships are "passthrough entities." The partnership doesn't pay an income tax, and each partner's share of income, deductions and credits for a tax year are reported to the partner on Schedule K-1. The partner reports his or her share of the partnership items on his or her individual income tax returns. The share of real estate rental income is reported on Schedule E, Part II.

Some states charge a fee or tax for the privilege of being a limited liability company. For example, in California, $800 is paid with the annual partnership income tax return.

The noncorporate owners might qualify for the federal tax deduction for business income not taxed to a C corporation. The income of a C corporation would be taxed at corporate income tax rates.

You can get Form 1065 and instructions; Publication 541, Partnerships, and Publication 1653, US Partnership Return of Income at the IRS web site, www.irs.gov.

Limited Liability Companies (LLCs)

For years, the IRS and business promoters fought over how entities should be taxed. Should an entity be allowed the benefits of passthrough taxation as a partnership, or subject to double taxation as a corporation?

---

86 IRC § 465(b)(6).

This was especially an issue for a relatively new type of entity, the limited liability company. For a limited liability company, all of the owners are supposed to receive the same type of liability protection as corporate shareholders.

Finally, the IRS took a "kinder and gentler" approach and offered businesses a choice in the "check the box" regulations.[87] The regulations became effective on January 1, 1997.

Under the check the box regulations, entities that are not incorporated under local law may elect to be taxed as a corporation or to be taxed as a pass-through entity. In some cases, such as a single-member LLC, the entity is disregarded entirely for income tax reporting.

LLCs were promoted by the legal profession to be an entity with limited liability protection for all of the owners (called "members") yet have the passthrough advantages of a partnership. Since qualified nonrecourse liabilities of a partnership pass through to owners with limited liability as additional investment for the purpose of claiming losses, LLCs are especially well-suited for holding real estate.

Some regular corporations would have liked to liquidate and convert to LLCs. In most cases this hasn't been possible, because the assets of the corporation would be deemed to be sold in a taxable liquidation, and the shareholders would have to report income for their shares of the corporate assets received.

There are still some unresolved issues for LLCs, including how the self-employment tax should apply to the earnings of the members. Some people have tried to apply the analogy of the limited partnership interest. Limited partners are not subject to self-employment tax on their shares of partnership earnings, but they are also prohibited from an active service role in the limited partnership. This prohibition doesn't apply to LLC members. I suspect this issue will eventually be resolved as Congress seeks more money to keep the Social Security system afloat without adopting a "tax increase."

Depending on the laws of the state in which they operate, LLCs may not conduct certain types of business. In California, real estate operations that don't require a state-issued license (in contrast to real estate brokers) are generally permitted.

Some states have special taxes and fees that apply to LLCs. For example, California has an $800 annual "privilege tax" plus a fee based on California-source gross receipts. In some cases, businesses have been structured as limited partnerships with an LLC general partner to minimize or eliminate the fee.

Since they are generally taxed as partnerships, LLCs have some advantages over S corporations, including the ability to have a non-resident of the United States as a member, the ability to have different types of "preferred" and "common" membership interests, and special allocations of income and deductions. They are also eligible for an election to adjust the basis of LLC assets relating to "outside" transactions, such as sales or inheritance of member interests. Liquidations of partnerships also generally result in minimal tax liability

---

87   Treasury Regulations § 301.7701.

to the members.

Again, as "partnerships," the net income of an LLC is generally not taxable to the LLC. A Schedule K-1 is provided to the members with their shares of income, deductions and credits for the taxable year. Members report their share of real estate operations at Schedule E, Part II.

LLCs are formed by registering with a Secretary of State for one of the states. LLCs are also registered with any state in which they are doing business. They are required to have a formal LLC agreement. LLCs aren't subject to some of the formalities of operation that corporations must follow to preserve liability protection for the members.

Noncorporate owners might qualify for the federal tax deduction for business income not taxed to a C corporation. The income of a C corporation would be taxed at corporate income tax rates.

You can get Form 1065 U.S. Partnership Income Tax Return and instructions; Form 8832, Entity Classification Election (check the box); Publication 541, Partnerships, and Publication 1653, US Partnership Return of Income at the IRS web site, www.irs.gov.

The Centralized Partnership Audit Regime

The IRS was experiencing difficulties handling the adjustments from audits of partnership income tax returns, because they require changes to income tax returns for each partner. Congress enacted a Centralized Partnership Audit Regime (CPAR) to simplify the audit adjustment process, effective for partnership income tax years beginning after 2017 and ending after August 12, 2018. It applies to most general partnerships, limited partnerships and limited liability companies taxed as partnerships.

The adjustments are generally taxed to the partnership at the maximum federal income tax rate. They are not passed through to the partners.

Certain partnerships with 100 or fewer qualified partners may elect out of CPAR.[88]

The following partners are not qualified partners:

(A) A partnership,

(B) A trust (including a revocable living trust),

(C) A foreign entity that is not an eligible foreign entity,

(D) A disregarded entity (such as a single-member LLC),

(E) An estate of an individual other than a deceased partner, or

(F) Any person that holds an interest in the partnership on behalf of another person.

---

88   Treasury Regulations § 301.6221(b)-1.

The details of CPAR are beyond the scope of this explanation, but you should discuss CPAR with your tax advisor when discussing choosing the form of doing business and the title of partnership interests.

Regular, or C Corporations

Regular corporations, also called C corporations (after Internal Revenue Code Subchapter C, which consists of most of the tax laws that apply to regular corporations), have the best-defined history of any of the limited liability entity forms.

The reason that corporations were created was to have a form of business where investment and ownership in the entity is separated from the management and operation of the entity. If corporate formalities are observed and there is no fraud, the liability of the investors is limited to the cash invested. Consult with a corporate attorney about the details.

The C corporation has the most flexibility in the types of ownership and investment available. For example, you can have voting common stock, non-voting common stock, preferred stock, bonds (debt instruments), convertible preferred stock, or convertible bonds.

Both U.S. residents and nonresidents can be owners. So can partnerships, LLCs, trusts, estates and other corporations.

When one corporation owns a majority of the stock in another, we say there is a parent-subsidiary structure.

C corporations are also taxed as separate entities from their owners (with the exception of consolidated groups). That's why we say they are subject to double taxation. Effective as of January 1, 2018, the corporate federal tax rate is 21% of taxable income. (Note this tax rate reduction is very simple compared to computing the deduction for business income of noncorporate taxpayers.) If the corporation pays dividends to its shareholders, they pay income taxes on the dividends they receive.

(Since lower corporate income tax brackets were repealed by the Tax Cuts and Jobs Act of 2017, some C corporations with lower income might actually pay higher income taxes under the Act.)

The low corporate income tax rate under the Tax Cuts and Jobs Act of 2017 is a powerful incentive to incorporate. It seems to me this rate will be the first target should the Democrats get control of Congress and the White House.

Currently, "qualified dividends" received by individuals, estates and trusts are subject to a maximum 20% federal income tax rate, plus a potential 3.8% federal surtax on net investment income.

There is currently no preferential tax rate for long-term capital gains of C corporations.

Capital losses of C corporations are only deductible to the extent of capital gains. They don't get the $3,000 additional annual allowance that other taxpayers do. Unused capital losses of C corporations may be carried back three years and forward five years. Other taxpayers don't have a carryback but have an unlimited carryover. No deduction is allowed for a capital loss carryback if it results in increasing a net operating loss.

For more details, you can get a copy of Form 1120, Schedule D and instructions at the IRS web site, www.irs.gov.

When a C corporation is liquidated, it is deemed to have sold its assets for fair market value. This means the corporation pays income tax for the deemed sale of the assets, then the shareholders pay income tax for the excess of the net assets received over the tax basis of their stock.

THE COMBINATION OF DOUBLE TAXATION, NO TAX RATE BREAK FOR LONG-TERM CAPITAL GAINS AND CAPITAL LOSS LIMITATIONS HAVE TRADITIONALLY MADE C CORPORATIONS A POOR CHOICE FOR HOLDING MOST REAL ESTATE INVESTMENTS. Lower corporate income tax rates under the Tax Cuts and Jobs Act of 2017 will motivate business owners to reconsider C corporations. The inability to liquidate the corporation without a double tax and the lack of a basis adjustment at death of the owners are also strong disincentives to incorporate. C corporations can be a good choice for real estate activities that generate ordinary income, such as new home developments.

Provided they are profitable, C corporations are superior to any other entity for providing tax-advantaged fringe benefits for owner-employees. For example, a C corporation can have a non-discriminatory medical reimbursement plan that pays the medical expenses of all employees. The corporation gets a tax deduction and the employees report no income for this benefit. Other "fringe" benefits for owner-employees, such as a company car, receive more favorable tax treatment in C corporations than for other entities.

Since retirement plan contributions of C corporations are based on W-2 (Medicare) income, they are much easier to calculate for C corporations than for partnerships or proprietorships (sole owners).

With a well-defined equity structure, C corporations are also the most straightforward of entities to administer for equity-based compensation arrangements, such as stock grants, incentive stock options, non-qualified stock options and ESOPs.

WITH THE ADVANTAGES OF C CORPORATIONS FOR LIMITED LIABILITY AND EMPLOYEE BENEFITS, REAL ESTATE INVESTMENTS ARE OFTEN STRUCTURED SO THE PROPERTY IS HELD BY AN INDIVIDUAL OR PASSTHROUGH ENTITY AND THE INDIVIDUAL OR ENTITY HIRES A C CORPORATION MANAGEMENT COMPANY. Also see Chapter 8 about passive activity losses. The management company can be owned by the same persons who own the real estate or who own interests in the passthrough entity.

You can get Form 1120 with instructions and Publication 542, Corporations, at the IRS web site, www.irs.gov.

S Corporations

Before the creation of limited liability companies, investors asked for an alternative that would reduce the double taxation disadvantage of C corporations. The S corporation alternative was created.

S corporations have a combination of characteristics of C corporations and partnerships.

S corporation shareholders who observe required operational formalities enjoy the same limited liability protection as C corporation shareholders.

An S corporation is only permitted to have one class of stock. This means owners' shares of stock are entitled to the same dividends and shares of income as other shareholders. No special allocations are permitted. Some variations of rights, such as the right of a shareholder vote, are permitted.

The only permitted shareholders are individuals, estates and certain trusts, banks, and certain exempt organizations. In addition, the shareholders must be citizens or residents of the United States. With so many nonresident alien investors who want to participate in buying U.S. real estate, this can be a problem.

The maximum number of shareholders is supposed to be limited to 100. There are rules that permit you to go beyond that number. For example, a husband and wife are counted as one shareholder. All qualifying members of a family who hold corporation stock are treated as one shareholder. I'm not going to go into the details of this exception here. Get professional tax advice to determine if your corporation has a qualification question.

A revocable living trust that is disregarded for income tax reporting purposes is also disregarded for qualification testing. The creator/owner of the trust is treated as directly owning the stock when the title is in the name of the trust. After the grantor's death, the trust is only permitted to own the stock for two years unless it makes a special election.

An S corporation can own a subsidiary. If an 100%-owned subsidiary makes an election to be a Qualified Subchapter S Subsidiary, it will be a disregarded entity and its income, deductions and credits will be reported on the parent's income tax returns.

S corporations generally don't pay a federal income tax. The shareholders' amounts of income, deduction and credits for a tax year are reported on Schedule K-1. The shareholders report these items on their individual income tax returns and pay the tax on the income. The shareholder's share of an S corporation's income from real estate operations is reported at Schedule E, Part II.

The S corporation rules favor corporations that have elected to be S corporations from inception.

For example, if a C corporation that holds appreciated property makes an S election, the gain from selling the property during the 5 years after the effective date of the election can result in a corporate-level built-in gains tax. (Originally the waiting period was 10 years. A temporary reduction of the waiting period to 5 years for 2012 and 2013 under the American Taxpayer Relief Act of 2012 and for 2014 under the Tax Increase Prevention Act of 2014 was made permanent under the Protecting Americans From Tax Hikes Act of 2015.)

Also, S corporations that have undistributed earnings from C corporation years can have a corporate-level tax when they have "excess net passive income." See your tax advisor for details. Be aware that *if an S corporation that has undistributed C corporation earnings and profits has excess net passive income for three consecutive years, the S election will automatically be terminated.*

Some states have a corporate-level tax that applies to S corporations. For example, California has an $800 minimum tax for each corporation, and 1.5% tax on corporate taxable income. Shareholders also pay income taxes on their shares of taxable income. Check the rules for your state. (Shareholders may be required to pay state income taxes for each state in which the S corporation has operations. The details are beyond the scope of this discussion. See your tax advisor.)

Distributions of income accumulated while the S election is in effect, called the accumulated adjustment account, is tax free to the shareholders, because they already paid tax on that income. The undistributed income is treated as an additional investment in corporate stock.

The tax basis of the shares must be recomputed annually to determine the amount of corporate losses that can be deducted. You start with the original cost of the stock, add shares of S corporation income items, subtract shares of S corporation deductions and shares of non-deductible expenses, subtract distributions made in previous years, and add additional amounts contributed.

Shareholder loans (loans from shareholders to the S corporation) are considered an additional investment in the S corporation when determining loss limitations. I recommend that you avoid making shareholder loans. Repaying demand loans from shareholders, including loans for which there is no written note, can result in taxable ordinary income to the shareholder/creditor.

Unlike partnerships and LLCs, loans by banks and other lenders to an S corporation aren't considered as an additional "investment" for S corporation shareholders, even if the shareholders guarantee the loan. This means S corporation shareholders aren't eligible to deduct their share of S corporation losses to the same extent that partners are eligible to deduct partnership losses.

If an S corporation is generating losses, the shareholders should meet before the year-end with their tax advisors to determine what actions should be taken to qualify for tax deductions. As I said before, avoid short-term loans from shareholders.

Like C corporations, S corporations are deemed to sell their assets when they are liquidated. This is a real problem when you want to continue holding real estate after a liquidation, because you will have to pay income tax as though the property was sold, but will not receive cash to pay the tax.

If S corporations have ordinary income from operations, such as from selling new homes in a housing development, the shareholders won't have to pay self-employment tax on undistributed income. The shareholder-employees and the corporation just pay Social Security and Medicare taxes on wages. (Watch for tax reform proposals attacking this "tax break.")

Because of this tax advantage, the IRS might claim that any amounts distributed to shareholder-employees should be treated as wages, especially for small S corporations when all of the shareholders are active in the business.

Like C corporations, qualified retirement plan contributions for S corporations are computed based on Medicare income reported on Form W-2. This makes administering retirement plans for S corporations much easier than for partnerships or proprietorships.

S corporations can have stock grant and stock option plans, but they are more difficult to administer than for C corporations because of the interaction of vesting the ownership of stock and the allocation of S corporation income to be reported on the shareholder-employee's Schedule K-1.

For other employee fringe benefits for shareholder-employees, limitations apply like those for partnerships. This means that some benefits, like medical reimbursement plans discussed for C corporations above, aren't available for S corporations.

Medical insurance premiums for shareholder employees are added to W-2 wages and deducted at line 16 on (2019) Schedule 1 of Form 1040, provided the premiums don't exceed wages plus distributed S corporation income or loss. If the allocated S corporation loss exceeds W-2 wages, the self-employed medical insurance won't be allowed as an "above the line" tax deduction.

Since you can avoid double taxation with an S corporation and get the benefit of individual long term capital gains rates, it can be a good choice in some circumstances. If the real estate operations are expected to generate losses, the inability to have S corporation debt counted as a shareholder "investment" for loss limitations is a significant disadvantage. If it's expected that real estate might be distributed in a future corporate liquidation, the immediate taxation of any appreciation of the property is another disadvantage. Since S corporations don't have as great employee benefit advantages as C corporations, they are not as good of a choice for a property management company.

The best use of an S corporation for real estate operations is probably for a real estate development, such as selling new homes.

Since owners of S corporations must be individuals or qualifying trusts, they might qualify for the federal tax deduction for business income not taxed to a C corporation.

You can get Form 1120 with instructions and Publication 542, Corporations (which includes an explanation about S corporations), at the IRS web site, www.irs.gov.

Real Estate Investment Trusts (REITs)

Another way that investors can join together to invest in real estate is to buy shares in a Real Estate Investment Trust, or REIT.

A REIT is like a mutual fund that invests in real estate and mortgages secured by real estate. It functions as a type of pass-through entity because the REIT is allowed to deduct dividends paid to its shareholders.

Unlike other passthrough entities, REITs can't pass through losses. This is a major disadvantage compared to other passthrough entities.

I am going to give a thumbnail explanation so that investors will understand how REITs operate. If you have any interest in creating and operating one, you will at least have to engage a CPA firm because most REITs are publicly traded. You should also have a tax specialist as an employee to be sure the quarterly compliance tests are met.

A REIT is formed as a corporation or an organization taxed as a corporation – often a "business trust." Since they are publicly traded corporations, there are no restrictions on who can own REIT shares.

REITs have evidences of beneficial ownership, which may be stock shares.

There must be at least 100 beneficial owners. More than 50% of the shares may not be owned, directly or indirectly, by five or fewer individuals at any time during the last half of the tax year.

The REIT must meet income and asset tests, requiring that essentially all of its income and assets relate to real estate and mortgages secured by real estate, but other temporary investments in marketable securities and cash are allowed.

The REIT must distribute almost all of its income to its shareholders. Like mutual funds, a REIT may elect to treat long term capital gains as deemed dividends that are treated as if they were distributed to the shareholders and reinvested in the REIT. The shareholders pay income taxes on the deemed dividends.

Long-term capital gains dividends are identified according to the special rates that apply, including 1) 20%/15% rate distributions, (2) unrecaptured Section 1250 gain subject to the 25% rate, and (3) 28% rate gain for collectibles and qualified small business stock.

REIT dividends attributable to qualified dividends (eligible for the 20% maximum tax rate) received by the REIT also qualify as qualified dividends for the shareholders who receive them. REIT dividends attributable to real estate operations or mortgage interest are not qualified dividends.

Shareholders of REITs who are individuals report long-term capital gains dividends on Schedule D, and other dividends on Schedule B.

Any REIT income that isn't distributed is taxed at corporate tax rates. (The corporate alternative minimum tax was repealed for tax years beginning after December 31, 2017 by the Tax Cuts and Jobs Act of 2017.)

If the REIT doesn't distribute enough of its income, penalties apply and the REIT could be disqualified, lose its status as a REIT and be prohibited from re-electing to be a REIT for five years.

Since REITs are formed for real estate *investment*, they can't conduct a trade or business, like a hotel, with the properties they own. They rent properties to operators.

Since REITs are corporations for tax purposes, they can grant stock options to their employees and offer employee benefits like C corporations.

The *Housing Tax Assistance Act of 2008*, enacted July 30, 2008, included several provisions to make it easier to operate REITs, especially for operations outside the United States. Since this is a brief introduction to REITs, I'm not going to give the details of those changes here. Ask your tax advisor if they are significant for your operations.

Since they are mostly publicly traded, advantages of REITs are (1) liquidity and (2) the single level of tax that applies to REIT earnings, including sales of real estate.

Noncorporate owners of REITs might qualify for the federal tax deduction for business income not taxed to a C corporation. The income of a C corporation owner would be taxed at corporate income tax rates.

You can get Form 1120-REIT with instructions at the IRS web site, www.irs.gov.

7

Depreciation and Cost Segregation

Depreciation is a critical deduction for real estate held for rental or for business. For many rental properties, total deductions for depreciation, interest and property taxes exceed the income from the property, resulting in a tax loss that may be limited.

What is depreciation? Taxpayers generally aren't allowed to deduct the tax basis (cost for determining gain and loss for income tax reporting) of assets that have a useful life of more than one year in the year placed in service. Instead, part of the tax basis is deductible each year over some period of time. The amount we get to deduct (or is shown as an expense on a financial statement) is called depreciation.

Since depreciation, insurance and maintenance are allowed as deductions for rental property but not for a personal residence, an individual might be able to afford owning an investment property held for rental even though he or she can't afford to own a personal residence.

For example, Jane Taxpayer owns a rental property. She receives $2,000 per month rent. For 20X1, her annual interest expense is $18,000, property taxes are $5,000 and insurance expense is $2,000. The property also has an annual depreciation deduction of $7,300.

Her tax loss is

Rent		$24,000
Interest	$18,000	
Property taxes	5,000	
Insurance	2,000	
Depreciation	7,300	
Total expenses		-32,300
Tax loss		-$8,300

If Jane can't take the loss under the passive activity loss rules (see Chapter 8), her rental income is still "sheltered" by her deductions, and she can carry the losses forward to apply against future income or to deduct when the rental property is sold.

Assume her principal payments for 20X1 were $2,000.

Assuming her tax loss is disallowed under the passive activity loss rules, here is her cash flow for the rental property:

Rent		$24,000
Total expenses	$32,300	
Less depreciation		
(non-cash expense)	-7,300	
Add principal payments	2,000	
Total cash disbursed		-27,000
Negative cash flow		-$3,000

Here is Jane's cash flow if she used the same home as a principal residence and therefore had no rental income,

Tax savings from deducting interest and property taxes at 32% ($18,000 + $5,000 = $23,000 X 32%)		$ 7,360
Payments		
Principal payments	$ 2,000	
Interest	18,000	
Property taxes	5,000	
Insurance	2,000	
Total cash disbursed		-27,000
Net negative cash flow		-$19,640

Since Jane can carry a rental property for a net $3,000 cash outflow compared to $19,640 if she bought a home to live in, you can see why many people get started in real estate as investors instead of as homeowners. (This obviously works most favorably if Jane lives with her parents and doesn't have to rent a place to live.)

Modified Accelerated Cost Recovery System (MACRS)

The current depreciation system for federal income tax reporting is called the Modified Accelerated Cost Recovery System, or MACRS.

There is no determination of "economic life" or "remaining economic life" required. You simply look up the depreciation rates on tables based on designated classes. (See IRS Publication 946, How To Depreciate Property.) A good feature of the system is to reduce or eliminate arguments with IRS agents over "useful lives." Before 1981, depreciation was one of the most common adjustments from income tax audits. Now depreciation-related arguments focus on the proper classification of property and whether maintenance or improvement expenditures should be capitalized or expensed. (See Chapter 10.)

MACRS was enacted as part of the Reagan-era Tax Reform Act of 1986.

Earlier depreciation rules still continue to be used for properties acquired before 1986 and when those properties are surrendered in a tax-deferred exchange. The old methods may still be used for the portion of the replacement property for which the tax basis is determined with reference to the surrendered property. See the section on tax-deferred exchanges and involuntary conversions below.

Some of the details for real estate depreciation, including bonus depreciation and the expense election, change over time. The rules that apply for a particular item of property or improvement are generally those for the year that it was placed in service. This is a good reason for hiring a tax professional to prepare your income tax returns. It's their job to keep track of current and historic tax rules.

Check your state tax rules about federal conformity. For example, California follows most of the federal tax depreciation rules for individuals (but not bonus depreciation and a lower (Section 179) expensing limit, and software is not depreciated but amortized in California), and California has not conformed to MACRS for regular corporations.

I am going to mostly focus on depreciation rules as they apply to real estate. For other issues, such as for computers, computer software and business-use vehicles, see IRS Publication 946, How To Depreciate Property, and IRS Publication 463, Travel, Entertainment, Gift and Car Expenses.

Section 179 Expense election.

Most real estate doesn't qualify for the Section 179 Expense election, except as described below and "qualified real property."

The Tax Cuts and Jobs Act of 2017 increased the federal expense election under Internal Revenue Code Section 179 from $510,000 for 2017 to $1,000,000. The current deduction for the Section 179 is limited to the taxable income, before the deduction, from any trade or business for the taxable year; any excess is carried forward to the next taxable year. The increase is effective for property placed in service in tax years beginning after December 31, 2017, and is adjusted for inflation for tax years beginning after December 31, 2018. Unless Congress takes further action, this limitation increase is permanent.

The inflation-adjusted limit for 2020 is $1,040,000.

(The eligible election amount is phased out when acquisitions of qualified property exceed $2.5 million for tax years beginning after December 31, 2017, adjusted for inflation. The inflation-adjusted threshold for 2020 is $2,590,000.)

In addition, the Act allows Section 179 expensing for property that is predominantly to furnish lodging or in connection with furnishing lodging. That means furniture in a rental home placed in service in tax years beginning after December 31, 2017 should qualify for the expense election.

Also effective for property placed in service in tax years beginning after December 31, 2017, the following improvements to nonresidential real property that are placed in service after that property was first placed in service also qualify for Section 179 expensing: (1) roofs; (2) heating, ventilation, and air conditioning property; (3) fire protection and alarm systems; and (4) security systems.

The portion of any property used for investment does not qualify for the expense election and doesn't qualify under the business use requirement.

Note that when a Section 179 expense election is made, the expensed amount is subject to recapture as *ordinary income* under Internal Revenue Code Section 1245. (See Chapter 2 – Other Sales of Real Estate.) This is a reason some taxpayers that made a Section 179 expense election for 2018 or 2019 might want to file an amended income tax return to change their election to bonus depreciation. See below.

Since the property for which a Section 179 expense election is reclassified to Section 1245 property subject to depreciation recapture, it appears to me it will not be like-kind property to Section 1250 depreciable real estate or land, so the gain in an exchange won't be eligible for exclusion under Section 1031.[89]

The expense election is applied before computing bonus depreciation. For qualified improvement property, bonus depreciation is an accelerated depreciation method for which the excess of the bonus depreciation over straight-line depreciation is subject to recapture as ordinary income under Internal Revenue Code Section 1250 when the property is sold (usually by the landlord).

Most of the differences to qualify for the expense election and for bonus depreciation have been eliminated by the Tax Cuts and Jobs Act of 2017. For the Section 179 election,

---

89   Internal Revenue Code § 1245(a)(3)(C).

the property must be used in a trade or business.[90] (This means property used for "production of income" in a rental operation doesn't qualify.) Property used outside the United States doesn't qualify for the expense election

Bonus depreciation.

Most real estate doesn't qualify for bonus depreciation, except for land improvements and qualified improvement property. See the explanation about qualified improvement property below in this chapter.

Property used in a rental operation can qualify for bonus depreciation. Property used outside the United States does not qualify.

The Tax Cuts and Jobs Act of 2017 increased the bonus percentage from 50% to 100%, effective for property acquired and placed in service after September 27, 2017 and before January 1, 2024. The percentage is phased down for property placed in service after December 31, 2023 until it will be zero for property placed in service after December 31, 2027. A taxpayer may elect to apply the 50% rate instead of the 100% rate for qualified property placed in service during the taxpayer's first tax year ending after September 27, 2017.

The Coronavirus Aid, Relief and Economic Security (CARES) Act (P.L. 116-136), enacted on March 27, 2020, included a technical correction defining "qualified improvement property" (see below) as 15-year MACRS property, effective for tax years beginning after 2017. This change makes qualified improvement property eligible for bonus depreciation.

The Tax Cuts and Jobs Act of 2017 also allows bonus depreciation for property used by an unrelated person effective for property placed in service after September 27, 2017.

Bonus depreciation applies automatically for any qualifying property acquired during a taxable year. A taxpayer may elect to not apply bonus depreciation on a class basis. For example, the election could be made for all 5-year MACRS property. If a taxpayer wants to be selective for claiming first-year depreciation, the taxpayer can elect out of bonus depreciation for a class, and then elect Section 179 expensing for selected items.

An advantage of bonus depreciation over Section 179 expensing is there is no trade or business income limit for bonus depreciation.

Remember that "taxes are on sale" under the Tax Cuts and Jobs Act of 2017. A taxpayer might decide to elect out of bonus depreciation and expensing to pay taxes at the low current federal tax rates.

De minimis expensing.

See the chapter on Materials and Supplies relating to whether the purchase of some items can be currently expensed based on a low cost. These items aren't applied against the expense election limitation, but a taxpayer might decide to use the expense election for them

90   IRC § 179(d)(1)(C).

as a protective measure.

Land v. improvements.

Land is not depreciable. The tax basis of real estate must be allocated to land and improvements using some reasonable method. I suggest that you should have an appraisal done to determine how the make the allocation. See also the section in this chapter on cost segregation studies.

Demolition of structure.

The costs of demolishing a structure are not tax deductible to either the owner or the lessee of real estate. The demolition costs are added to the tax basis of the land for the property where the structure was located.[91]

A modification or rehabilitation of a building will not be considered a demolition provided (1) 75% or more of the existing external walls of the building are retained as internal or external walls and (2) 75% or more of the existing internal structural framework of the building is retained in place.[92] In this case, the modifications or repairs may be added to the cost of the building or expensed as repairs, as appropriate.

If a building is acquired with the intent to demolish and it is used for business or income-production for a short time before it's demolished, a portion of the cost basis not to exceed the present value of the right to receive rentals during the period of its expected use may be allocated to the building and depreciated over that period.[93]

Depreciation rules for different classes of assets.

Residential real estate is depreciated over 27.5 years on a straight-line basis with a half-month convention. (A half-month convention means one-half the depreciation for one month is claimed for the month the property is placed in service and one-half month for the final month of its useful life or when it is disposed of.) That means the same depreciation will be claimed for most years. For example, a year's depreciation for a residential building that cost $275,000 would be $10,000. One-half month of depreciation is claimed in the month the property is placed in service and one-half month for the month the property is sold.

Non-residential or commercial real estate is depreciated over 39 years on a straight-line basis, with a half-month convention. For example, a year's depreciation for a commercial building that cost $390,000 would be $10,000.

For real estate placed in service after 1999, there is no alternative minimum tax difference for depreciation on residential and commercial buildings.

Another depreciable category for real estate is land improvements. Land improvements

91	IRC § 280B.
92	Revenue Procedure 95-27, 1995-1 CB 704.
93	Treasury Regulations § 1.165-3(a)(2)(i).

include a broad list of items, such as sidewalks, concrete driveways, parking lots, fences, landscaping, underground plumbing, underground drainage systems, and playground equipment. Some land improvements are not depreciable, such as demolition costs (discussed above) and some land preparation costs.

Depreciable land improvements are depreciated using a 15-year period on a 150% declining-balance method in earlier years, converting to straight-line in later years. The general rule is a half-year convention applies for the year the asset is placed in service and the year sold. If more than 40% of property eligible for accelerated depreciation is placed in service during the last three months of a taxable year, a mid-quarter convention applies. The IRS has issued proposed Treasury Regulations that clarify depreciable land improvements as like-kind real estate to land and buildings qualifying for a like-kind exchange.[94] (See Chapter 5.) They are Section 1250 property, so the excess of the MACRS deduction or bonus depreciation over straight-line depreciation for land improvements is subject to recapture at sale as ordinary income. (See Chapter 2.)

The IRS has tables where you can look up the depreciation percentages for a tax year, provided the property has only been used in 12-month tax years.

The lives for other assets are determined by reference to an IRS table. This table was derived from a previous system, called the Alternative Depreciation System or ADS. It was mostly designed for large industrial companies, such as manufacturers, energy exploration companies, telephone companies and power generation companies. Sometimes it's hard to tell what life and convention to apply.

Automobiles, computers and computer peripherals are five-year property. The IRS has ruled that items used in residential rental property, including stoves and refrigerators, furniture, carpets, blinds and window treatments are five-year property.[95] Five-year property is depreciated on a 200% declining balance method in the early years, converting to straight-line in later years. The half-year convention generally applies, but the mid-quarter convention applies if the 40% test mentioned for 15-year property is failed.

Office furniture, fixtures and equipment used in a property management office are seven-year property. Seven-year property is depreciated on a 200% declining balance method in the early years, converting to straight-line in later years. The half-year convention generally applies, but the mid-quarter convention applies if the 40% test mentioned for 15-year property is failed. In some cases, all or part of a building is an integrated part of the manufacturing process, and so may be eligible for depreciation as manufacturing equipment.

Depreciation of leasehold improvements is generally computed disregarding the term of the lease. If a lessee abandons the improvements at the end of the lease, the lessee computes loss (or gain) based on the undepreciated basis of the improvements.

A landlord does not report income for improvements made by a lessee that become

---

94   REG-117589-18, June 12, 2020.
95   Announcement 99-82, 1999-2 CB 244.

the lessor's property at the termination of the lease. This rule does not apply when the improvements represent the liquidation of lease rentals or for improvements that are made in lieu of rental income.[96]

The lessor is also allowed to claim a loss (or gain) for any improvements made by the lessor with respect to a lease that are disposed of at the termination of the lease.

Effective for tax years beginning after December 31, 2017, certain real property trade or businesses that elect out of interest deduction limits must use the alternative depreciation system (ADS) for residential rental property, nonresidential real property and qualified improvement property. Under the ADS system, depreciation is computed using the straight-line method over 30 years (as amended) for residential rental property, 40 years for nonresidential real property, or 20 years for qualified improvement property. See the explanation about qualified improvement property below.

Qualified improvement property.

As a simplification measure, Congress combined certain real estate improvements as one category in the Tax Cuts and Jobs Act of 2017, called qualified improvement property, effective for property placed in service after December 31, 2017. The intention of Congress was for qualified improvement property to be assigned a 15-year MACRS life, using straight-line depreciation. The 15-year life would qualify the property for bonus depreciation and Section 179 expensing. Unfortunately, Congress made a drafting error that originally subjected this property to a 39-year life as nonresidential real estate.

The Coronavirus Aid, Relief and Economic Security (CARES) Act (P.L. 116-136), enacted on March 27, 2020, included a technical correction defining "qualified improvement property" (see below) as 15-year MACRS property, effective for tax years beginning after 2017.

The IRS has issued guidance for changing the accounting method for depreciation to conform to the technical correction, which generally would be to claim bonus depreciation or to claim straight-line depreciation with a 15-year life and a half-year or mid-quarter convention. The alternative depreciation system life is 20 years. The correction can be made on an amended return, administrative adjustment request for a partnership, or a Form 3115, Application for Change in Accounting Method, to change the depreciation of qualified improvement property placed in service after December 31, 2017 in the taxpayer's 2018, 2019, or 2020 taxable year. The taxpayer may also make a late election to waive bonus depreciation. See the guidance for details.[97]

Qualified improvement property is any improvement to an interior portion of a building which is nonresidential real property if the improvement is placed in service after the date the building was first placed in service by a taxpayer. Qualified improvement does not include expenditures for (1) the enlargement of a building; (2) an elevator or escalator;

---

96   Treasury Regulations § 1.109-1.
97   Revenue Procedure 2020-25.

or (3) the internal structural framework of a building.

This definition is similar to a previous one under Internal Revenue Code Section 168(k)(3) for bonus depreciation, which has been repealed.

The eligibility of external improvements to a restaurant for bonus depreciation that applied before 2018 has been repealed. When these improvements are made after 2017, they will be depreciated as 39-year nonresidential real property.

The property classifications and 15-year recovery periods for qualified leasehold, retail and restaurant improvements were repealed, effective for improvements placed in service after December 31, 2017.

Foreign-use property

Property used outside the United States must be depreciated using the Alternative Depreciation System, or ADS.[98] This means the property must be depreciated using the straight-line method. In some cases, the lives over which the property must be depreciated are longer than under MACRS. For non-residential buildings, the life is 40 years. For residential rental property, the Tax Cuts and Jobs Act reduced the ADS life from 40 to 30 years. Since I am mostly focusing on U.S. operations in this book, I'm not going to discuss ADS in detail. See IRS Publication 946. You can get a copy at www.irs.gov.

Alternative minimum tax

For property placed in service after December 31, 1998, an AMT adjustment is made for property depreciated under MACRS for 3, 5, 7 and 10-year property depreciated using the 200% declining-balance method or Section 1250 property depreciated using a method other than the straight-line method.

The AMT depreciation is computed using a 150% declining balance method in the early years, converting to straight-line in later years. The IRS has provided tables for computing the annual depreciation allowances.

In the early years, the difference is added back to the income for the related activity. In the later years, the AMT depreciation will be greater than the regular tax depreciation, and will be subtracted from the income for the related activity.

There is no depreciation adjustment for the building (27.5 year or 39 year straight line), for land improvements (15 year, 150% declining balance converting to straight line in later years), or for qualified leasehold improvements (15 years straight-line).

Cost segregation studies

As we have seen, there are significant differences in depreciation depending on the classification of the property.

---

98   IRC § 168(g)(1)(A).

In some cases, some parts of the real estate improvements may qualify for depreciation over shorter periods than the "default" amounts for buildings, and for accelerated depreciation methods.

One example we have already mentioned is land improvements.

Another is electrical improvements installed specifically for certain equipment items, like a copy machine or computer equipment. These improvements can be depreciated based on the term of the supported equipment (7 or 5 years).

Making an allocation of building costs to the correct categories requires a building engineer. Many companies now specialize in making these "cost segregation studies." *This is not a job for an amateur.*

It can be worthwhile to hire one of these companies when a building is being designed and constructed to plan for qualifying as many of the costs as possible for more depreciation in earlier years.

The IRS issued an Audit Techniques Guide during January 2005 that does a good job of explaining this process. The Cost Segregation companies use the Audit Guide as a guideline for their services. You can get a copy of the Audit Techniques Guide at the IRS web site, www.irs.gov. In the "search" box, key "audit guide cost segregation."

A cost segregation study can even be done in later years and a "catch up" adjustment made for depreciation that could have been claimed in earlier years.

If the deductions from the property are limited by the passive activity loss rules, you may not receive sufficient tax benefits to recover the fees for the cost segregation study and for preparing the paperwork for the IRS for the change.

Another concern is qualifying for a like-kind exchange. In order to qualify for tax deferral, the property received must be like kind to the property surrendered. Proposed Treasury Regulations for Section 1031 tax deferred exchanges are fairly liberal in classifying some of the items with shorter depreciable lives as real property. (See Chapter 5.) Personal property items that are not classified as real property are not eligible for an exchange under Internal Revenue Code Section 1031. Cost segregation studies may be required for both the property given up and the acquired property at the time of the exchange.

Also remember that accumulated depreciation in excess of straight-line depreciation for buildings is subject to Section 1250 recapture as ordinary income. This means part of the gain may be taxed at a higher income tax rate (currently 35% compared to 25% for unrecaptured Section 1250 gain).

If you expect to make frequent exchanges or a sale in a relatively short time (say 10 years), you probably shouldn't have a cost segregation study done.

Tax-deferred exchanges and involuntary conversions

Making the computations and establishing new depreciation schedules for property received in a tax-free exchange or an involuntary conversion is a very involved process. This is another area where getting help from a qualified tax advisor is definitely worth the investment.

I am only going to give a brief summary of some of the rules here.

The IRS has issued detailed regulations about how to depreciate replacement property received in a tax-deferred exchange or in an involuntary conversion.[99] The regulations only apply when both the property surrendered and property received are depreciated using MACRS.

The IRS MACRS depreciation tables probably won't work for the replacement property.

The tax basis for the property received is divided into two pieces (if applicable). One piece is the tax basis, called depreciable exchanged basis, which is determined with reference to the (depreciable) surrendered property. The other piece, called depreciable excess basis, is the tax basis determined with reference to other amounts paid for the property.

No depreciation is claimed during the period between when the property was surrendered and when the replacement property was received.[100] The depreciation is suspended during this period.

Depreciation of the depreciable exchanged basis.

If the depreciation methods and lives are the same for the replacement property as for the surrendered property, the undepreciated tax basis of the surrendered property is depreciated over the remaining life of surrendered property, starting when the replacement property is placed in service.[101] For example, Property A is exchanged for Property B. Both properties are residential rental properties. Property A was acquired on January 1, 2000. Property A was surrendered on February 29, 2008. Property B was received on July 1, 2008. The undepreciated basis for Property A was $100,000. (Remember, a half-month convention applies.) Property A was depreciated for 97 months, or 8 years and 1 month. That leaves a remaining life of 19 years and 5 months or 229 months for Property B. Depreciation will start for property B on July 1, 2008. The monthly depreciation will be $100,000 / 229 = $437, with one-half month or $218 for July 2008.

If the replacement property has a longer recovery period than the surrendered property, the undepreciated tax basis is depreciated using the remaining life determined

---

99   Treasury Regulations § 1.168(i)-6.
100   Treasury Regulations § 1.168(i)-6(c)(5)(iv).
101   Treasury Regulations § 1.168(i)-6(c)(3)(ii).

as if the surrendered property had the same recovery period.[102] Using the facts in the previous paragraph but assuming the replacement property is a non-residential building and the surrendered property was a residential building, the remaining life for computing depreciation would be 39 years – 8 years and one month = 30 years and 11 months or 371 months. One month's depreciation would be $270 and the depreciation for July 2008 would be $135.

If the replacement property has a shorter recovery period than the surrendered property, the property is depreciated over the *(longer)* remaining life for the *surrendered property*.[103]

Depreciation of the depreciable excess basis.

Any depreciable excess basis in the replacement MACRS property is treated as property placed in service by the acquiring taxpayer at the time of replacement.[104] For example, if Jane Taxpayer surrendered Building A for Building B, which is residential real estate, plus paid an additional $100,000 during 2008, the $100,000 amount would be depreciated over 27.5 years, as if she had purchased another building for that amount.

Property surrendered wasn't depreciated using MACRS.

If property that was not depreciated under MACRS (say acquired in 1980) is surrendered for property that is depreciated under MACRS, the assigned net tax basis (tax basis less accumulated depreciation) for the surrendered property is depreciated as property placed in service by the acquiring taxpayer at the time of replacement. For example, if John Taxpayer exchanged a building acquired in 1980 with an undepreciated basis of $50,000 for a residential rental building in 2008, the $50,000 amount would be depreciated over 27.5 years, as if he had purchased another building for that amount.[105]

Election to not apply rules for replacement property.

The taxpayer may elect to not apply the rules in the regulations relating to the replacement property. This means a remaining life would not be used for computing the MACRS deduction for the replacement property.[106] The election would be to a taxpayer's advantage if a non-residential building that was in service for a short time was exchanged for a residential building.

Facilitative costs

Under repair and capitalization regulations issued by the IRS on September 13, 2013, certain expenses that facilitate the acquisition of property must be capitalized. These are amounts paid in the process of investigating or otherwise pursuing an acquisition.

102	Treasury Regulations § 1.168(i)-6(c)(4)(i).
103	Treasury Regulations § 1.168(i)-6(c)(4)(ii).
104	Treasury Regulations § 1.168(i)-6(e)(3).
105	Letter Ruling 8929047, April 25, 1989.
106	Treasury Regulations § 1.168(i)-6(i).

Here is a list of inherently facilitative items that are required to be capitalized when incurred in the process of investigating or pursuing the acquisition of real or personal property.[107]

1. Transporting property;

2. Securing an appraisal or determining the value or price of property;

3. Negotiating the terms or structure of the acquisition and obtaining tax advice on the acquisition;

4. Application fees, bidding costs, or similar expenses;

5. Preparing and reviewing the documents that effectuate the acquisition of the property;

6. Examining and evaluating the title of property;

7. Obtaining regulatory approval of the acquisition or securing permits related to the acquisition, including application fees;

8. Conveying property between the parties, including sales and transfer taxes and title registration costs;

9. Finder's fees or brokers' commissions, including contingency fees;

10. Architectural, geological, survey, engineering, environmental, or inspection services pertaining to particular properties; or

11. Services provided by a qualified intermediary or other facilitator of an exchange under Section 1031.

Under a special rule for acquisitions of real property, amounts other than inherently facilitative costs paid by a taxpayer in the process of investigating or otherwise pursuing the acquisition of real property aren't considered to facilitate the acquisition if they relate to activities performed in the process of determining whether to acquire real property and which real property to acquire.[108]

Amounts paid for employee compensation and overhead are treated as amounts that do not facilitate the acquisition of real or personal property. (These expenses are required to be capitalized for self-produced property or property acquired for resale.)[109]

#

107	Treasury Regulations §1.263(a)-2(f)(ii).
108	Treasury Regulations §1.263(a)-2(f)(iii).
109	Treasury Regulations §1.263(a)-2(f)(iv).

For additional information, see Form 4562 (Depreciation and Amortization) with instructions; IRS Publication 527, Residential Rental Property; IRS Publication 544, Sales and Other Dispositions of Assets; IRS Publication 551, Basis of Assets; and IRS Publication 946, How to Depreciate Property. You can get them at the IRS web site, www.irs.gov.

8
At Risk Limitation, Passive Activity Loss Limitation and Excess Business Loss Limitation

Once the amount of a loss for a real estate activity is established under income tax accounting rules, there are additional "hoops" to be passed before the loss can be deducted from other taxable income: the at-risk limitations, the passive activity loss limitation, and the excess business loss limitation. The excess business loss limitation was enacted in the Tax Cuts and Jobs Act of 2017, effective for tax years beginning after December 31, 2017 and before January 1, 2026.

At Risk Limitation

I have already summarized the at-risk limitation as it applies to the various forms of real estate operations in Chapter 6.

Losses from a trade or business or a rental activity conducted for the production of income are limited to the "investment" in the activity.

The "investment" consists of cash plus the tax basis of assets contributed to the activity plus liabilities that are treated as additional investment amounts. Generally, in order for liabilities to be treated as an investment amount, the taxpayer has to be personally liable to pay them, or "at risk." Personal loans to an LLC, a partnership or an S corporation also count as "at risk" investment amounts. The limitation based on the investment amount is adjusted each year to add additional amounts invested, reinvested profits, increased owner loans and increases in "at risk" liabilities; and to subtract distributions of assets, losses, payments on owner loans and decreases in "at risk" liabilities.

(Payments on owner loans that have been used under the At Risk Limitations to allow the deduction of losses result in taxable income. I generally discourage making these loans.)

The determination of the At-Risk Limitation amount is done each year on Form 6198.

Any loss that is disallowed under the At-Risk Limitations is carried forward to the next taxable year. If there is a profit or an increase in the investment in the activity for the next year, the loss may be allowed at that time. Any previously disallowed losses "disappear" when the activity is sold. The reason is allowed losses reduce the tax basis of the property. Gains on sale do not represent an additional investment, so suspended at-risk losses aren't allowed to offset the gains or other income.

There is a special benefit for the activity of holding real estate that allows "qualified nonrecourse financing" to be included as an investment under the At Risk limitations. These limitations enable limited partners and LLC members to deduct bigger losses than they otherwise would be able to, subject to the passive activity loss limitations.

Qualified nonrecourse financing is any financing which is (1) secured by real property used in the activity, (2) borrowed by a taxpayer with respect to the activity of holding real property, (3) provided by organizations in the business of lending for which no one is personally liable and secured by real estate used in the activity. The organizations include banks, savings and loan associations, credit unions, insurance companies, pension trusts, and government agencies. Loans guaranteed by federal, state or local government agencies also qualify.

Limited partners and LLC members receive an allocated share of the "investment" from qualified nonrecourse financing based on the theory that, since no one is personally liable for the debt, everyone should participate.

S corporation shareholders do not receive any "at risk" investment for their shares of corporate liabilities because of the liability protection of the corporate form. This rule applies even if the shareholders personally guarantee payment of a corporate liability.

Passive Activity Loss Limitations

The passive activity loss (PAL) limitations represent one of the most complex areas of the tax law. Defining passive activities has become even more significant with the enactment of the 3.8% tax on net investment income, or net investment income tax. See chapter 14 for more discussion.

To understand why we have the PAL limitations, we have to go back to when they were enacted in 1986. In 1986, the U.S. tax system was in danger of collapse. Tax shelters, which at one time were used almost exclusively by the highest-income taxpayers, were actively being marketed by the personal financial planning industry to the middle class. Our income tax system was becoming an elective system. You could decide not to pay income taxes by participating in a tax shelter.

The goal of the Reagan Administration was to save the U.S. tax system by reducing the maximum income tax rate from 50% for earned income to 25%. In order to do that, it would have to increase the base of income that income taxes applied to. The main ways the broader base was accomplished was by (1) decreasing some income tax deductions, such as by having longer depreciation lives (real estate was depreciated over 15- and 18- year periods before the Tax Reform Act of 1986), (2) eliminating some tax deductions, such as for consumer interest, and (3) limiting tax deductions for rental operations and trades or businesses that a taxpayer wasn't "actively participating" in, which included most tax shelters.

These goals were accomplished in the Tax Reform Act of 1986. The nominal maximum tax rate was 28%. The above changes were adopted. Such a major "mid-stream" change has consequences, and we suffered from them. The Savings and Loan industry, commercial real estate, the financial planning industry, and most tax sheltered investments collapsed. There was a major adjustment in our economy. Our tax system has had more integrity since the passive activity loss limitations were adopted.

After the Reagan Administration, we have experienced a gradual restoration of tax-favored investments and higher tax rates. Under the Trump Administration, we have seen further reductions in tax deductions and a reduction in tax rates. Unless Congress takes further action, most of the Trump initiated changes will expire after 2025.

I will only discuss some highlights of the rules for passive activity losses here. Since passive activity loss limitations can apply differently for regular tax and alternative minimum tax reporting and for federal and state reporting, you should use a professional tax return preparer for your income tax returns if these rules apply to you.

The passive activity loss rules apply to individuals, estates and trusts. They also apply to personal service corporations, certain regulated investment companies (REITs and mutual funds), and certain "C" corporations more than 50% owned by five or fewer individuals. Those "C" corporations are allowed to deduct the losses against "net active income," but not portfolio income (royalties, dividends and interest). Since losses pass through to the partners of partnerships, members of most limited liability companies, and shareholders of S corporations, passive activity information is reported on the information returns for these entities.

In applying the passive activity loss limitations, income and losses are segregated into three "baskets": (1) earned income (mostly wages and active trade or business income); (2) portfolio income (mostly from interest and dividends, but some types of income that would otherwise be passive are categorized as portfolio income, explained below); and (3) passive income and losses. Passive losses are generally not deductible against earned and portfolio income until the activity is disposed.

A passive activity is either (1) an activity that involves the conduct of a trade or business in which the taxpayer does not materially participate or (2) a rental activity, regardless of whether the taxpayer participates in the activity.

The basic rule for passive activity losses is when a taxpayer doesn't actively participate in a trade or business or an income-producing activity, losses from the activity are only currently deductible up to the amount of passive activity income from other activities. Any disallowed losses are suspended and carried forward to the next year. When the activity is sold or otherwise disposed of, suspended losses from that activity will be deductible for the year of sale or disposition.

Tax credits from passive activities can also be limited. Any remaining disallowed credits when the activity is disposed of are not allowed, but the taxpayer may elect to restore any basis adjustments relating to disallowed credits.

The limitations are computed on Form 8582, Passive Activity Losses, and Form 8582-CR, Passive Activity Credits. You can get these forms at the IRS web site, www.irs.gov.

What are separate activities?

The taxpayer has some latitude in determining what a "separate activity" is. The regulations allow grouping activities as an "appropriate economic unit."[110] However, rental activities generally may not be grouped with trade or business activities unless they are otherwise an appropriate economic unit and (1) the rental activity is insubstantial in relation to the trade or business activity; (2) the trade or business activity is insubstantial in relation to the rental activity; or (3) each owner of the trade or business activity has the same proportionate ownership interest in the rental activity, in which case the portion of the rental activity that involves the rental of items of property for use in the trade or business activity may be grouped with the trade or business activity.[111]

There are two concerns about identifying separate activities.

1. Annual accounting for the passive activity loss limitations by activities. The more activities, the more complex the accounting.

2. When an activity is disposed, any suspended losses with respect to the activity are allowed. If the activity is broadly defined, losses will continue to be suspended when a major operation is disposed.

There is a provision to help reduce the impact of the second concern. When there is a disposition of a substantial part of an activity, the taxpayer may treat the interest disposed of as a separate activity.[112] In order to use this exception, the taxpayer must be able to establish with reasonable certainty the amount of gross income, deductions and credits allocable to that part of the activity for the tax year, including suspended amounts carried forward from prior tax years. Meeting this requirement for the exception may be practically impossible.

Rental real estate activities.

Rental real estate activities are generally treated as passive.

There is an exception where up to $25,000 of losses from certain rental real estate activities may be deducted currently. The $25,000 limitation is reduced by 50¢ for each $1 of modified adjusted gross income over $100,000. This means when modified adjusted gross income exceeds $150,000, none of the losses are currently deductible. In order to qualify for the $25,000 allowance, the taxpayer must "actively participate," own at least 10% of the activity, and not be a limited partner. (These limitations are cut in half for married persons, filing separately.)

(Hotels and motels that rent rooms to transients are not rental real estate activities but are trades or businesses. If the taxpayer materially participates in the hotel or motel trade or business, the losses will be deductible and not subject to the passive activity loss limitations.)

---

110   Treasury Regulations § 1.469-4(c).
111   Treasury Regulations § 1.469-4(d).
112   Treasury Regulations § 1.469-4(g).

Real estate professionals.

A special rule allows a taxpayer to treat rental real estate activities in which he or she materially participates as nonpassive activities (not subject to the limitations) provided more than half of the personal services the taxpayer performs in trades or businesses during the tax year are performed in real estate trades or businesses *and* he or she performs more than 750 hours of services during the tax year in real estate trades or businesses. For a joint return, either spouse can separately satisfy the requirements. This rule "trumps" the $25,000 exclusion for certain taxpayers with income below a certain level (discussed above).

If you are claiming to meet these requirements, you should keep a detailed daily diary of your activities. If you have another occupation, such as a dentist or medical doctor, the chances of defending "real estate professional" status are remote, unless your spouse qualifies. (See below.)

Note that qualifying as a real estate professional is a threshold to meet an exception from real estate rental activities automatically being considered passive activities. The taxpayer still must meet the material participation requirement for the properties in order for them to be considered non-passive. For example, a taxpayer can qualify as a real estate professional by working more than 750 hours as a real estate agent and meeting the other tests. The same taxpayer must have also worked more than 500 hours on his or her rental real estate in order to qualify the activity as non-passive.[113]

The material participation tests are required to be applied for each real estate activity as a separate activity, but the taxpayer may elect to treat all interests in rental real estate as one activity. (This is an election that is often missed or misplaced. Keep a copy in your permanent file.) Publicly-traded partnerships are not included in the election to treat all interests in rental real estate as one activity.

Real property trades or businesses include real property development, redevelopment, construction, reconstruction, acquisition, conversion, rental, operation, management, leasing, or brokerage trades or businesses.

Personal services as an employee are not counted as performed in real property trades or businesses unless the employee owns at least 5% of the employer.

Real estate professional status is effective for a joint income tax return if either spouse qualifies.

The Tax Court has ruled that a trust can qualify as a real estate professional. The activities of the trustees in a family real estate business were sufficient to qualify the trust.[114]

The IRS is aggressively auditing tax returns for which real estate professional status is claimed and has been successfully litigating the issue in Tax Court. Be prepared to defend yourself (or your client). Due diligence is essential.

---

113 *Gragg v. Commissioner*, 2014-1 USTC ¶ 50,245, April 4, 2014.
114 *Frank Aragona Trust*, 142 T.C. No. 9, March 27, 2014.

Some states, including California, have not adopted the real estate professional exception, so the passive activity loss limitation will apply to real estate rental activities in those states.

Election to treat all rental properties as one activity.

As a relief measure, Congress enacted a special rule for taxpayers in certain real property businesses.

Qualifying taxpayers may elect to treat all interests in rental real estate as one activity.[115]

By making this election, a taxpayer can count all of the hours of participation in the various properties to meet the requirements to be a real estate professional. (More than one-half of personal services performed in real property trades or businesses and more than 750 hours performed in real property trades or businesses in which the taxpayer materially participates. Either spouse can qualify for a joint income tax return.)

Notice the election is made for "rental real estate". Some real estate activities are not considered rental real estate and don't qualify for the election. For example, short-term rental of a vacation property for average periods of seven days or less during a taxable year is not considered rental for this purpose. If significant personal services are provided on behalf of the owner of the property in connection with making the property available to customers (like a hotel), the ineligible average short-term rental period is 30 days or less.[116]

Once the election is made, it continues in effect. You will want to keep a permanent record of the election and when it was made. As a precaution, some taxpayers include the election on their income tax return each year.

Note that some states, including California, haven't adopted this rule, so rental real estate might be non-passive on a federal income tax return but not on the state income tax return for the same taxpayer in the same tax year.

Rental of nondepreciable property.

If less than 30% of the unadjusted basis of a property is subject to a depreciation allowance, it is deemed to be "nondepreciable property" and any otherwise passive net income from the property is recharacterized as nonpassive portfolio income.[117]

Net income from rental to related entity.

Income from property rented to a partnership, S corporation or C corporation in which the taxpayer materially participates is nonpassive.[118]

---

115   Internal Revenue Code § 469(c)(7).
116   Treasury Regulations § 1.469-1T(e)(3)(ii), *Eger et al v. U.S.*, No. 19017022, 9th Circuity August 10, 2020.
117   Temporary Treasury Regulations § 1.469-2T(f)(3).
118   Treasury Regulations § 1.469-2(f)(6).

Self-charged interest.

A portion of interest income from a loan to a passive activity by a person who owns direct or indirect interests in the entity may be recharacterized as passive activity income.[119] Interest income from a loan from one passive activity to another that have identical ownership can also be recharacterized as passive activity income.

Rental of residence.

The rental of a dwelling unit used as a residence by the taxpayer during the tax year is not a passive activity for the tax year.[120]

Material participation.

For trades or businesses (not rental real estate operations), the taxpayer must materially participate in an activity in order to avoid being subject to the passive activity loss limitations. The taxpayer must materially participate on a regular, continuous and substantial basis.

The IRS has specified in temporary regulations that a taxpayer may meet one of six tests to be considered materially participating:[121]

(1) The taxpayer participates in the activity for more than 500 hours during the tax year.

(2) The taxpayer's participation constitutes substantially all of the participation in the activity of all individuals (including nonowners) for the tax year.

(3) The taxpayer participates in the activity for more than 100 hours during the tax year, and his/her participation is not less than the participation of any other person.

(4) The activity is a "significant participation" activity for the tax year, and his/her aggregate participation in all significant participation activities during the year exceeds 500 hours. A significant participation activity is one in which the taxpayer has more than 100 hours of participation during the tax year but fails to satisfy any other test for material participation. (Rental activitie aren't counted.) If the total of all the time spent in significant participation activities exceeds 500 hours, the activities are considered nonpassive.

(5) The taxpayer materially participated in the activity for any five tax years of the 10 tax years immediately preceding the tax year at issue.

(6) The activity is a personal service activity and he/she materially participated in the activity for any three tax years preceding the tax year at issue.

119	Treasury Regulations § 1.469-7.
120	Temporary Treasury Regulations § 1.469-1T(e)(5).
121	Temporary Treasury Regulations § 1.469-5T.

The taxpayer may also show material participation based on the facts and circumstances, but must have participated in the activity for more than 100 hours.

Management services of an owner are disregarded in meeting the material participation tests, unless (1) no person except the individual at issue, who performs management services for the activity, receives compensation in consideration of the services and (2) no individual performs services in connection with the management of the activity that exceed (by hours) the amount of the management services performed by the individual at issue.

Proving your "hours of participation" in an activity may be difficult unless you keep a daily diary – especially if you are involved in several different businesses.

Limited partners.

Limited partnership interests are generally passive activities.[122] However, a limited partner who meets tests (1), (5) or (6) under "material participation" will be considered to materially participate.[123] Also, a limited partner that also is a general partner in the partnership will be considered to be a general partner for an entire taxable year for both interests for that year.[124]

Limited liability company members.

The Tax Court and Federal Claims Court have ruled that members of a California LLC should be treated as general partners because they are allowed under state law to participate in management of the LLC.[125] The IRS has issued Prop. Reg. § 1.469-5(e)(e)(i) that would accept this position, provided the holder of the interest has rights to manage the entity.

Publicly-traded partnerships.

The passive activity losses of a publicly-traded partnership may only be deducted against the income from that particular partnership and not against passive activity income from other activities.[126] You should know if a partnership you invested in is publicly traded, but there is a box D at Part I of Form 1065, Schedule K-1 that should be checked if the partnership is publicly traded.

Passive assets and estate tax deferral.

There is an estate tax election relating to whether real estate is involved in an active trade or business, but the rules are quite different from the passive activity loss rules that apply for income tax reporting.

---

122 IRC § 469(h)(2).
123 Temporary Treasury Regulations § 1.469-5T(e)(2).
124 Temporary Treasury Regulations § 1.469-5T(e)(e)(ii).
125 *Garnett v. Commissioner*, 132 TC 368, *Newell v. Commissioner*, TC Memo 2010-23, *Thompson v. United States*, USTC 2009-2 ¶ 50,501.
126 IRC § 469(k).

The due date for payments of estate tax attributable to a "closely held business" may be postponed (no payments due) for up to five years and then the estate tax payments may be made in up to 10 equal installments.[127] Further, the interest that applies to the postponed tax is computed at favorable rates. The rate is only two percent for the first $1,000,000 in value, indexed for inflation after 2000. The indexed amount for 2020 is $1,570,000. The rate for the balance of the tax attributable to a closely held business is 45% of the rate that applies to underpayments of tax.[128] No deduction is allowed for this interest for either estate tax or income tax reporting.[129]

The election must be made on a timely-filed estate tax return, including extensions of time to file.

To qualify for the election, the closely-held business must exceed 35% of the adjusted gross estate. An interest in a closely held business means (1) an interest as a proprietor in a trade or business; (2) an interest in a non-publicly traded partnership carrying on a trade or business, provided 20% of the total capital interest of the partnership is included in determining the gross estate of the decedent, or the partnership had 45 or fewer partners; or (3) stock in a non-publicly traded corporation, provided 20% or more in value of the voting stock of the corporation is included in determining the gross estate of the decedent, or the corporation had 45 or fewer shareholders.

"Passive assets" that aren't used in carrying on a trade or business aren't eligible for the election.

More than one business can be aggregated in order to qualify for the election.

If more than 50% of the ownership interest in a closely held business for which the election was made is disposed of, then the unpaid portion of the tax attributable to that business will become due.

In addition, if the estate has undistributed net income for any taxable year ending on or after the due date for the first installment (five years and nine months after death), the balance of the deferred estate tax must be paid on the due date for the income tax return for the taxable year that includes that due date. Therefore, the executor or trustee must assure that the accumulated income of the estate is distributed on time to avoid disqualification.

The good news is the IRS has issued guidance on the qualification of real estate for the election to postpone payment of estate tax at favorable interest rates, and said the definition of non-passive assets is quite different from the income tax passive activity loss rules.[130] If the taxpayer is responsible for negotiating leases, management, and repair of the property, the operation can qualify as a closely-held business. Also, if the property is leased to a partnership or corporation that qualifies as a closely-held business for the decedent, the

---

127   IRC § 6166.
128   IRC § 6601(j).
129   IRC §§ 163(k) and 2053(c).
130   Revenue Ruling 2006-34.

operation of the property by the partnership or corporation is aggregated with the operation by the decedent, making it much easier to qualify.

If you are planning to qualify for this election, you don't want to delegate the operation of the property to a management company that doesn't qualify as a closely-held business (meeting the requirements for this election) and you don't want to have a triple-net lease to a business that doesn't qualify as a closely-held business.

This is only an introduction to this subject for further discussion with your tax advisor and your estate planning attorney.

Excess business losses of noncorporate taxpayers

Effective for tax years beginning after December 31, 2017 and before January 1, 2026, taxpayers other than C corporations were scheduled to be subject to another limitation on deducting business losses, called "excess business losses."[131]

The Coronavirus Aid, Relief and Economic Security (CARES) Act (P.L. 116-136), enacted on March 27, 2020, retroactively suspends the excess business loss limitation for taxable years beginning after December 31, 2017 and before January 1, 2021. Taxpayers who applied the limitation for 2018 and 2019 should amend their income tax returns to claim the losses.

The limitation is part of a sequence of limitations: (1) basis, (2) at risk, (3) passive activities, and (4) excess business losses.

An excess business loss is the excess, if any, of the taxpayer's aggregate deductions for the tax year from the taxpayer's trades or businesses over (1) the taxpayer's aggregate gross income or gain for the tax year from the trades or businesses plus (2) $250,000 ($500,000 for married, filing a joint return) to be adjusted annually for inflation.

Any amount disallowed under this limitation is added to the taxpayer's net operating loss carryover and subject to the deduction limitation for net operating losses. For tax years beginning after December 31, 2017, net operating losses for tax years beginning after December 31, 2017 were scheduled to be limited to 80% of taxable income of the carryover year, before the net operating loss deduction.[132] (Most net operating loss carrybacks were repealed by the Tax Cuts and Jobs Act of 2017.)

Passthrough income and losses from partnerships and S corporations are included in the computation for excess business losses.

The CARES Act suspends and liberalizes the net operating loss rules for taxable years beginning after December 31, 2017 and before January 1, 2021. Net operating losses may be carried back 5 taxable years. The 80% of taxable income limitation for deducting net operating loss carryovers has been suspended. Taxpayers may elect to waive the carryback.

131	Internal Revenue Code Section 461(l).
132	Internal Revenue Code Section 172(b).

There is also a special election available to excluded carrybacks to one or more years that have income exclusion of offshore income under Internal Revenue Code Section 965.

Taxpayers could revoke a previous election to waive a net operating loss carryback by July 25, 2020.

The IRS has issued guidance about handling the net operating loss changes in the CARES Act in Revenue Procedure 2020-24.

In Notice 202-26, the Department of the Treasury and the IRS granted a six-month extension of time to file Form 1045 or Form 1139 to taxpayers that have a net operating loss that arose in a taxable year that began during 2018 and ended on or before June 30, 2019.

#

For more details, see IRS Publication 925, Passive Activity and At-Risk Rules. Also see IRS Form 461 and instructions, Limitation on Business Losses, used to report Excess Business Losses. The limitation has been suspended for 2018, 2019 and 2020 by the CARES Act. You can get the form and instructions for 2018 and 2019 at the IRS web site, www.irs.gov, under Forms and Instructions – Prior Years to study it and prepare for the limitation when it is reinstated for 2021.

9
Deducting Mortgage Interest

Probably the most common errors on income tax returns involving real estate are the presentation and amounts of mortgage interest deductions.

Just deduct the interest for the mortgages secured by your principal residence and a second residence as itemized deductions on Schedule A and the interest for mortgages secured by rental properties on the schedule of income and deductions for the properties on Schedule E, right? Probably wrong.

The main source of the errors is the routine practice of refinancing properties, taking cash out "tax free," and using the funds for other purposes, including buying other properties. In most cases, this practice brings a requirement for interest tracing into play.

The tax deduction limitations for mortgage interest for a principal residence have been reduced under the Tax Cuts and Jobs Act of 2017.

In this chapter, I'll briefly outline some of the rules that apply to deducting mortgage interest. After you read it, there's a good chance that you'll decide to have a tax consultant familiar with these rules prepare your income tax returns.

Types of interest

Under the income tax laws, there are different types of interest, subject to different limitations.

Personal interest is not tax deductible.

Interest for the acquisition or improvement of a principal residence or a second residence and secured by that residence is deductible as an itemized deduction on Schedule A, and is also deductible when computing the alternative minimum tax. Effective for tax years beginning after December 31, 2017 and before January 1, 2016, the maximum debt for which this deduction may be claimed is $750,000, or $375,000 for a married person filing a separate income tax return. That limitation applies for acquisition debt incurred after December 15, 2017. Under a grandfather rule, the maximum debt for which this deduction may be claimed for debt incurred before December 16, 2017 is $1 million, or $500,000 for a married person filing a separate income tax return. The grandfather rule also applies to the limitation amount for refinanced mortgages. (For example, if a grandfathered mortgage with a balance of $800,000 is refinanced after 2017 with a principal balance of $900,000, $800,000 of the replacement mortgage would be qualified indebtedness.)

Mortgage insurance premiums in connection with qualified acquisition indebtedness may be deductible as mortgage interest. The deduction is only allowed for mortgage insurance contracts issued after December 31, 2006, and unless Congress takes action, the deduction will expire after 2020. Amounts paid during 2020 that are allocable to a period after 2020 aren't deductible. The deduction is phased out by 10% for each $1,000 ($500 for married persons filing a separate return) that the taxpayer's adjusted gross income for the taxable year exceeds $100,000 ($50,000 for married persons filing a separate return).[133] (The sunset date was extended by H.R. 1865, Further Consolidated Appropriations Act, 2020.)

Under the Tax Cuts and Jobs Act of 2017, the deduction for "equity indebtedness" is repealed for tax years beginning after December 31, 2017 and before January 1, 2026. The deduction is scheduled to be reinstated after 2025. Interest for "equity indebtedness" of up to $100,000, secured by a principal residence or a second residence was deductible as an itemized deduction on Schedule A, but could be disallowed as personal interest when computing the alternative minimum tax. Since interest expense for equity indebtedness was reported differently for the alternative minimum tax, a portion of the interest could be deductible as investment interest for the alternative minimum tax, with the limitation computed on a separate AMT Form 4952 (see below). An example of personal interest disallowed for AMT would be borrowing money on an equity line of credit to buy a car. The $100,000 limit for equity indebtedness was in addition to the $1 million limit for qualified residential housing interest.

Investment interest is deductible up to the amount of investment income. The limitation is computed on Form 4952. You can get the form at www.irs.gov.

Business interest is generally deductible as an expense on the related form: Schedule C for a trade or business, Schedule E for a rental property, or Schedule F for a farm. Depending on the circumstances, losses from these operations may be subject to the passive activity loss limitations. (See Chapter 8.) Also, interest expense is not deducted, but capitalized when property is under construction.

What is a qualified indebtedness for the acquisition or improvement of a residence?

Qualified acquisition indebtedness is a debt that is (1) incurred in acquiring, constructing, or substantially improving a qualified residence of a taxpayer, and (2) secured by that residence.[134] (If you refinance a residence to buy another residence, that debt won't be qualified acquisition indebtedness.)

The total amount of acquisition indebtedness for a residence may not exceed the cost of the residence, including improvements.[135]

The residence may be the principal residence of the taxpayer and a second residence, which can be selected by the taxpayer for each tax year.[136]

133	IRC § 163(h)(3)(E).
134	IRC § 163(h)(3)(B)(i).
135	Treasury Notice 84-74.
136	IRC § 163(h)(4)(A).

See the explanation above about the maximum indebtedness for which an itemized deduction may be claimed for residential mortgage interest.

Any debt secured by a qualified residence that was incurred before October 13, 1987 or a refinancing of such debt is covered by a grandfather rule. That debt qualifies as acquisition indebtedness and is not subject to the $750,000 or $1,000,000 limit.[137] However, the $750,000 or $1,000,000 limit for other debt is reduced by the outstanding amount of pre-October 13, 1987 indebtedness.

Here are the general rules to determine whether the debt qualifies:[138]

1. The proceeds are used to buy, construct or substantially improve the residence. Tracing rules beyond the scope of this explanation are used to determine how the proceeds were used. I recommend either paying the expenses directly using an equity line of credit or depositing refinancing proceeds in a separate bank account and paying for improvements from that account. You can also use this rule to make financing that didn't qualify, such as debt secured by another property to purchase or improve a qualifying residence, into qualifying indebtedness by using refinancing proceeds secured by the qualifying residence to pay off the other debt.

2. Debt incurred within 90 days before or after the date of purchase. The amount of the qualifying debt is the lesser of the amount of the debt or the purchase price.

3. Debt incurred up to two years before completion of construction or improvements. The amount of the qualifying debt is the lesser of the amount of the debt or the amount spent on construction. Only amounts spent on construction during the two-year period before the date the debt is incurred are counted.

4. Debt incurred up to 90 days after completion of construction or improvement. The amount of qualifying debt is the lesser of the amount of the debt or the amount spent on the construction. Only expenditures within the period starting two years before the completion and ending on the date the debt is incurred are counted.

The date the debt is incurred is generally based on when the loan proceeds are disbursed, usually the closing date. The debt may also be treated as incurred on the date a written application is made for the loan, provided the loan proceeds are disbursed within a reasonable time after approval of the application.

---

137   IRC § 163(h)(3)(D).
138   Treasury Notice 84-74.

What happens when you refinance a mortgage secured by a qualified residence?

When you refinance a mortgage secured by a qualified residence, you are supposed to trace where the funds are used. This can be done most easily by depositing any loan proceeds in a separate account and paying the desired expenses from that account. The interest is then prorated into different categories according to the use of the funds. The IRS has issued fairly liberal regulations that let you allocate principal repayments most favorably for yourself.

For example, say you refinanced your home. Using a $500,000 loan, you paid off the mortgage balance of $300,000 from when you bought the home. $150,000 is used to remodel the home. $50,000 is used to buy a new car. Initially, interest will be allocated 90% as qualified residential housing interest and 10% as home equity interest. Since the home equity interest isn't tax deductible, you can allocate principal payments first to that balance until it's eliminated. Then all of the interest on the mortgage balance after the home equity piece is paid off will be residential housing interest.

What if you refinance your home for $500,000, paid off the $300,000 mortgage balance from when you bought the home, and used $200,000 to buy a second residence? Since the $200,000 loan isn't secured by the second residence, the interest paid would not be residential housing interest. Under the current tax rules, interest with respect to $200,000 would be non-deductible personal interest. If you later refinanced the second residence and used the proceeds to pay off $200,000 of the mortgage on the principal residence, interest on the new mortgage would be tax deductible as residential housing interest because it would be funds used to purchase the residence and secured by that residence.

Refinancing rental properties

What happens when you refinance a rental property and use the cash elsewhere? This is commonly done as a way to get "tax-free" cash without selling a property.

You are supposed to trace how the funds are used and deduct the interest accordingly.

For example, you refinance property A for a new $500,000 mortgage. $300,000 of the proceeds is used to pay off the original acquisition mortgage. $100,000 is used to buy rental property B. $100,000 is used to remodel your principal residence. 60% of the interest is deductible on Schedule E for property A. 20% of the interest is deductible on Schedule E for property B. Since the mortgage isn't secured by the principal residence or a second residence, 20% of the interest attributable to remodeling your principal residence is non-deductible personal interest.

Refinancing through passthrough entities

Accounting can get even more complicated when properties are refinanced through passthrough entities. When the loan proceeds are passed through as distributions to partners or S corporation shareholders, the interest is separately reported and each partner or shareholder is required to allocate the interest according to how the funds were used. You should definitely get professional help when applying the rules for passthrough entities. Even better – avoid making loans to make distributions to partners or shareholders.

With the combination of the explosions of investments in real estate and refinancing of real estate, accounting for mortgage interest will become a big tax audit issue. Avoid having a big bill for taxes due plus interest and penalties by making the effort to correctly report your interest deductions on your income tax returns. Get professional help.

Points

Points paid for purchasing a principal residence are currently deductible (subject to the $750,000 or $1 million mortgage limit). This includes the portion of points that are paid for refinancing that are attributable to funds used to pay for a major home improvement. Note the points must be *paid* in order to get the current deduction. If they are added to the loan or paid using loan proceeds, the points are deducted as they are paid over the term of the loan. An "original issue discount" computation should be made to determine when the points are paid.

Points for financing other than the purchase or improvement of a principal residence are amortized over the term of the loan. Any unamortized amount is usually deductible when the mortgage is paid off, unless it is refinanced with the same lender.

Limitation on deduction for business interest

The Tax Cuts and Jobs Act of 2017 enacted a new limitation on the deduction for business interest.[139] Unlike previous limits that only applied to C corporations, the new limitation applies to all taxpayers.

The general rule is the deduction for business interest for any taxpayer is limited to the sum of:

- business interest income of the taxpayer for the tax year;
- 30% of the taxpayer's adjusted taxable income for the year, including any increases in adjusted taxable income as a result of a distributive share in a partnership or S corporation, but not below zero; and
- floor plan financing interest expense of the taxpayer for the tax year.

The Coronavirus Aid, Relief and Economic Security (CARES) Act (P.L. 116-136) enacted on March 27, 2020 increased the threshold from 30% to 50% for tax years beginning in 2019 and 2020.[140]

---

139   Internal Revenue Code § 163(j).
140   Internal Revenue Code § 613(j)(10).

Adjusted taxable income is regular taxable income, excluding:
- any item of income, gain, deduction or loss that is not properly allocable to a trade or business;
- any business interest expense or business interest income;
- any net operating loss deduction;
- the 20% deduction for qualified business income of a passthrough entity; and
- For tax years beginning before January 1, 2022, any allowable deduction for depreciation, amortization or depletion.

The limitation applies to certain taxpayers that have more than $25 million of business income or are "tax shelters".

The limitations are applied for partnerships (including LLCs taxed as partnerships) and S corporations at the entity level and the income of partnerships and S corporations isn't counted for the threshold of the owners.

Any disallowed interest expense deduction is carried forward to the next tax year, except partnerships and S corporations distribute the disallowed interest to their owners to carry forward on the owner's income tax returns and deduct based on income distributed by the partnership or S corporation in a succeeding tax year.

A taxpayer may elect to exclude from the limitation any real property trade or business as defined under the passive activity loss rules. This includes a real estate development, redevelopment, construction, reconstruction, acquisition, conversion, rental, operation, management, leasing or brokerage trade or business. The election is irrevocable.

It seems that making this election would be a "no brainer," except there are side effects. A taxpayer who elects to be excluded from the limitation for deducting business interest expense must use the alternative depreciation system (ADS) for nonresidential real property, residential rental property, and qualified improvement property held by the electing real property trade or business. This means qualified improvement property is ineligible for bonus depreciation and must be depreciated using straight-line depreciation for twenty years. The ADS lives for nonresidential real estate is 40 years and for residential real estate is 30 years. (See Chapter 7.)

If the business interest expense for the taxpayer is below the 30% or 50% limit, there is no need to make the election.

I don't expect most readers of this book to have this much income. If you do, you should definitely work with a professional tax advisor who is familiar with the rules to prepare your income tax returns.

The IRS has issued final regulations for the business interest limitation.[141] My printout is 574 pages. I can't cover all of the details here. The IRS has also issued proposed

---

141 TD 9905.

regulations covering the changes in the CARES Act.[142] Your tax advisor should study them.

#

For more information, see IRS Publication 527, Residential Rental Property, and IRS Publication 936, Home Mortgage Interest Deduction, Form 8990 and instructions, Limitation on Business Interest Expense Under Section 163(j). You can get them at the IRS web site, www.irs.gov.

---

142   REG-107911-18.

10
Repairs – Current Deduction or Capitalized?

Historically, a big area of controversy and disagreement between the IRS and taxpayers for real estate operations is whether repairs are currently deductible or should be capitalized and possibly depreciated.

The stakes are high. If the repair is made to the building and it must be capitalized and depreciated, the deductions will be spread over 27 ½ years for residential real estate and 39 years for commercial real estate. If the repair is capitalized as a land improvement, the deductions will be spread over 15 years. There is a possibility of currently deducting qualified improvement property using an expense election or as bonus depreciation. See Chapter 7 and your tax advisor for current developments. Obviously, the immediate tax benefit of a current deduction is more valuable than depreciation of a capitalized cost.

The IRS undertook a huge project and issued final regulations relating to repairs and capitalization on September 13, 2013.[143] These rules are now effective and must be followed for tax return reporting.

The good news is the IRS listened to comments made by the tax return preparation community and adopted several taxpayer-friendly simplification rules.

Although the regulations clarify many issues, judgment is also required when applying them, which means there is still room for disputes with the IRS.

Because these rules are complex, I recommend consulting with a tax advisor who is familiar with them when making major repairs for business property.

Books bigger than this one will be devoted to repairs and capitalization. I can only hit a few highlights here, emphasizing items that relate to real estate. Investors should get professional advice and professional advisors should study the Treasury Regulations, revenue procedures and other rulings and IRS guidance.

New safe harbor for "small taxpayers"

One of the most helpful provisions of the new repair and capitalization regulations is a safe harbor election for certain "small taxpayers."

If the requirements are met, the taxpayer may elect to expense amounts paid for repairs, maintenance, improvements and similar activities, even if they would otherwise be

---

143   T.D. 9636, September 13, 2013.

required to be capitalized.[144]

The election can only be made if the total of the expenses does not exceed the lesser of (1) 2% of the unadjusted basis of the eligible building property; or (2) $10,000.[145]

If the total amount of the expenses exceeds the threshold, the election isn't available.[146] The threshold amounts for the maximum expenses and gross receipts can be modified through published guidance issued by the IRS.[147]

In computing the limitation, the total expenses include amounts not capitalized under the de minimis safe harbor (see the chapter 13) and the safe harbor for routine maintenance.[148]

In order to qualify as a "small taxpayer," the taxpayer's average gross receipts for the three preceding taxable years may not exceed $10,000,000. Adjustments are made for short tax years. Gross receipts are generally not reduced by the cost of goods sold, but sales of property used in a trade or business are reduced by the taxpayer's adjusted basis in the property. Sales tax collected generally isn't included in gross receipts.[149]

In order to qualify for the election, the unadjusted basis for the building for which the expenses are incurred may not exceed $1 million.[150]

The unadjusted basis for an eligible building leased to a taxpayer is the total amount of rent, without discounting to present value, paid or expected to be paid by the lessee over the entire term of the lease, including renewal periods if it is reasonably expected the lease will be renewed.[151]

The election is made by attaching a statement to the taxpayer's timely-filed (including extensions) federal income tax return for the year the expenses are paid. The details of what must be included are in the regulations. S corporations and partnerships make their own elections, not the shareholders or partners. This isn't an accounting method for which a change of accounting method form is required to be filed. Change of accounting method forms can't be used to make a late election. A late election can be made on an amended return after getting the IRS's consent to make a late election.[152]

---

144   Treasury Regulations §§ 1.263(a)-3(h)(1), 1.263(a)-3(h)(7).
145   Treasury Regulations § 1.263(a)-3(h)(1).
146   Treasury Regulations § 1.263(a)-3(h)(8).
147   Treasury Regulations § 1.263(a)-3(h)(9).
148   Treasury Regulations § 1.263(a)-3(h)(2).
149   Treasury Regulations § 1.263(a)-3(h)(3).
150   Treasury Regulations § 1.263(a)-3(h)(4).
151   Treasury Regulations § 1.263(a)-3(h)(5)(ii).
152   Treasury Regulations § 1.263(a)-3(h)(6).

Once made, the election is irrevocable.[153]

If the taxpayer qualifies, this will be an election that whoever prepares the income tax returns will need to remember to make each year.

Safe harbor for routine maintenance

Another relief measure in the new repair and capitalization regulations allows a current tax deduction for "routine maintenance." This is not an elective provision, but the taxpayer may elect to capitalize these expenses.[154]

For a building, routine maintenance includes recurring activities that a taxpayer expects to perform to keep the building structure or systems (see below) in ordinarily efficient operating condition. Routine maintenance activities include the inspection, cleaning, and testing of the building structure or each building system, and the replacement of damaged or worn parts with comparable and commercially available parts. The activities are routine only if the taxpayer reasonably expects to perform the activities more than once during the 10-year period beginning at the time the building structure or building system upon which the routine maintenance is performed is placed in service by the taxpayer. The taxpayer merely has to substantiate its expectation, it doesn't have to actually perform the maintenance a second time during the 10-year period. A lessor's use of a building includes the lessee's use of the property.[155]

For property other than buildings, routine maintenance is the recurring activities that a taxpayer expects to perform as a result of the taxpayer's use of the property to keep the property in its ordinarily efficient operating condition. Routine maintenance activities include the inspection, cleaning, and testing of the property and the replacement of damaged or worn parts with comparable and commercially available parts. The activities are routine only if, at the time the property is placed in service by the taxpayer, the taxpayer reasonably expects to perform the activities more than once during the class life of the property. The taxpayer merely has to substantiate its expectation, it doesn't have to actually perform the maintenance a second time during the class life period. A lessor's use of property includes the lessee's use of the property.[156]

Routine maintenance doesn't include the following:[157]

1. Amounts paid for a betterment to a unit of property (explained below);

2. Amounts paid to replace a component of a unit of property when the taxpayer has properly deducted a loss for the component (other than certain casualty losses);

---

153   Treasury Regulations § 1.263(a)-3(h)(6).
154   Treasury Regulations § 1.263(a)-3(n).
155   Treasury Regulations § 1.263(a)-3(i)(1)(i).
156   Treasury Regulations § 1.263(a)-3(i)(1)(ii).
157   Treasury Regulations § 1.263(a)-3(i)(3).

3. Amounts paid to replace a component of a unit of property for which the taxpayer has properly taken into account the adjusted basis of the component in realizing gain or loss from the sale or exchange of the component;

4. Amounts paid for the restoration of damage to a unit of property for which the taxpayer is required to take a basis adjustment as a result of a casualty loss or casualty event;

5. Amounts paid to return a unit of property to its ordinarily efficient operating condition if the property has deteriorated to a state of disrepair and is no longer functional for its intended use;

6. Amounts paid to adapt a unit of property to a new or different use;

7. Amounts paid for repairs, maintenance or improvement of network assets, such as railroad track, oil and gas pipeline, water and sewage pipeline, power transmission and distribution lines, and telephone and cable lines that are owned or leased by taxpayers in each of those industries;[158]

8. Amounts paid for repairs, maintenance or improvement of rotable and temporary spare parts to which the taxpayer applies the optional method of accounting for rotable or temporary spare parts.

Amounts paid for routine maintenance might still have to be capitalized to improvements or inventory if they are direct or allocable indirect costs of other property produced by the taxpayer or property produced or acquired for resale.[159]

If the maintenance relates to the use of a previous owner for used equipment, it doesn't qualify as routine maintenance and has to be capitalized.[160]

Building systems

The improvement rules are applied separately to each of nine building systems and to the building structure.

The nine building systems are:

1. Heating, ventilation and air conditioning (HVAC) systems
2. Plumbing systems
3. Electrical systems

---

158 Treasury Regulations § 1.263(a)-3(e)(3)(iii).
159 Treasury Regulations § 1.263(a)-3(i)(5).
160 Treasury Regulations § 1.263(a)-3(i)(6) Example 4.

4. Escalators
5. Elevators
6. Fire protection and alarm systems
7. Security systems
8. Gas distribution systems
9. Other structural components specifically designated as building systems in future published guidance

Leased buildings

For lessees that lease an entire building, the unit of property is the building and the improvement rules are applied to the building systems and structure as if the building was owned by the lessee.[161]

A lessee is not required to capitalize improvements to the extent it receives a construction allowance for the purpose of the improvement or to the extent the improvement is a substitute for rent.[162]

A lessor is required to capitalize amounts that it pays directly or indirectly through a construction allowance, or when the lessee's improvement is a substitute for rent.[163]

It may be that improvements made aren't building improvements, but personal property, such as for retail displays.

Repairs done before a building is placed in service

Repairs that would ordinarily be deductible after a building is placed in service, such as painting, are required to be capitalized when performed before it is placed in service. These items are considered to be amounts incurred to acquire the building.[164]

Repairs incidental to improvements

All of the direct and indirect costs of an improvement must be capitalized, including otherwise deductible repair costs that directly benefit or are incurred because of an improvement.[165]

Removal costs

If a taxpayer disposes of a depreciable asset or component and has taken into account the adjusted basis of the asset in determining gain or loss, then the costs of removing the component or asset are not required to be capitalized. If the disposal is not a disposition for federal tax purposes, then the removal cost may be deductible or have to be capitalized based on whether the removal costs directly benefit or are incurred because of a repair or an improvement to the unit of property.[166]

---

161 Treasury Regulations § 1.263(a)-3(e)(2)(v).
162 Treasury Regulations § 1.263(a)-3(f)(2).
163 Treasury Regulations § 1.263(a)-3(f)(3).
164 Treasury Regulations § 1.263(a)-2(d)(2), Example 11.
165 Treasury Regulations § 1.263(a)-2(g)(1)(i).
166 Treasury Regulations § 1.263(a)-2(g)(2).

Repairs to residence incidental to improvements (remodeling)

A taxpayer who is an individual may capitalize amounts paid for repairs and maintenance made at the same time as capital improvements to a residence if the amounts are paid relating to improving (including remodeling) the residence.[167]

Personal and other real property

For personal property and real property other than a building, all of the components that are functionally interdependent are considered to be a single unit of property. The improvement rules are applied at the unit of property level.[168]

This means that an item like an automobile can't be segregated into an engine, body, muffler, driveshaft and tires.

A component can be treated as a separate unit of property if its depreciation period or method is different than the unit of property of which it is a part in the year that unit of property is placed in service.[169] For example, tires used on transport industry trucks are depreciated over a five-year period and the trucks are depreciated over a three-year period.[170]

Improvements that must be capitalized

Improvements must be capitalized if they are betterments, restorations, or adapt the property to a new or different use.[171]

An improvement is a betterment if it (1) ameliorates a material condition or defect that either existed before the taxpayer's acquisition of the property or arose during the production of the unit of property; (2) is for a material addition, including a physical enlargement, expansion, extension or addition of a major component or a material increase in the capacity; (3) is reasonably expected to materially increase the productivity, efficiency, strength, quality, or output of the unit of property.[172] For a building, the evaluation of whether an improvement is a betterment is made for improvements to the building systems and structure.[173]

An example in the regulations is the installation of a rubber roof membrane over an existing membrane that has started to leak. The existing membrane was in good condition when the taxpayer placed it in service. In this case, the amount paid to add the new membrane isn't a material addition, and the cost is currently deductible.[174]

167	Treasury Regulations § 1.263(a)-2(g)(1)(ii).
168	Treasury Regulations § 1.263(a)-3(e)(3)(i).
169	Treasury Regulations § 1.263(a)-3(e)(5)(i).
170	Treasury Regulations § 1.263(a)-3(e)(6), Example 16.
171	Treasury Regulations § 1.263(a)-3(d).
172	Treasury Regulations § 1.263(a)-3(j)(1).
173	Treasury Regulations § 1.263(a)-3(j)(2)(ii).
174	Treasury Regulations § 1.263-3(j)(3) Example 13.

An improvement restores a unit of property if it (1) is for the replacement of a component of a unit of property for which the taxpayer has properly deducted a loss for the component, other than a casualty loss; (2) is for the replacement of a component of a unit of property for which the taxpayer has properly taken into account the adjusted basis of the component in realizing gain or loss resulting from the sale or exchange of the component; (3) is for restoring damage to a unit of property for which the taxpayer is required to take a basis adjustment as a result of a casualty loss under Internal Revenue Code Section 165; (4) returns the unit of property to its ordinarily efficient operating condition if the property has deteriorated to a state of disrepair and is no longer functional for its intended use; (5) results in the rebuilding of the unit of property to a like-new condition after the end of its class life; (6) is for the replacement of a part or a combination of parts that comprise a major component or a substantial structural part of a unit of property.

The regulations include an example of a building that has an HVAC system comprised of three furnaces, three air conditioning units and duct work. One of the furnaces breaks down, and the taxpayer replaces it with a new furnace. In this case, the single furnace is not considered to be a significant portion of the HVAC system, so replacement of the furnace is not a restoration, and therefore the cost may be currently deductible.[175]

In another example, an HVAC system includes one chiller unit that breaks down. In this case, the chiller unit performs a discrete and critical function in the operation of the system, since it is the cooling mechanism for the whole system. The replacement of the chiller system is a restoration and must be capitalized.[176]

A taxpayer must capitalize an improvement paid to adapt a unit of property to a new or different use. It is a new or different use if it isn't consistent with the ordinary use of the property at the time the unit was originally placed in service.[177]

In an example, a manufacturing building is converted to a showroom. Structural components are removed and replaced for a better layout. The building interior is repainted. In this case, the improvements relate to adapting the building to a new or different use and must be capitalized.[178]

In another example, a building is repainted and the hardwood floors refinished to prepare to sell the building. This is not an improvement that is required to be capitalized.[179]

Note that repairs might have to be evaluated under more than one of the standards as a betterment, restoration or adaptation.

When applying these rules, I recommend that the taxpayer or tax advisor study all of the examples in the regulations to better understand how to apply the rules.

175	Treasury Regulations § 1.263-3(k)(7) Example 16.
176	Treasury Regulations § 1.263-3(k)(7) Example 17.
177	Treasury Regulations § 1.263-3(l)(1).
178	Treasury Regulations § 1.263-3(l)(3) Example 1.
179	Treasury Regulations § 1.263-3(l)(3) Example 3.

Election to capitalize repair and maintenance costs

A taxpayer may elect to treat amounts paid during a taxable year for repair and maintenance as capital expenditures if the taxpayer incurs the amounts in carrying on the taxpayer's trade or business and the taxpayer treats the amounts as capital expenditures on its books and records.

The election is made annually on the taxpayers timely-filed original income tax returns.

The election doesn't apply to repairs or maintenance of rotable or temporary spare parts to which the taxpayer applies the optional method of accounting (not detailed in this book).

Since this is an annual election, it isn't a change in accounting method.

Partial dispositions

In the past, taxpayers weren't able to claim losses for partial dispositions of an asset, such as when a roof was replaced. In order to deduct the undepreciated cost of a building, the entire building had to be sold.

The IRS has issued proposed and temporary regulations that would allow a taxpayer to elect to make such a deduction.[180] The rules are generally proposed to be effective for taxable years beginning on or after January 1, 2014.

The proposed regulations include provisions relating to general asset accounts (GAAs) that are beyond the scope of this explanation. A taxpayer may not elect to recognize a loss relating to the retirement of a structural component of a building held in a GAA, so some taxpayers might decide to revoke their general asset account elections.[181]

Automatic procedures are included in Revenue Procedure 2014-17 to do this when the GAA election was made in 2012 or 2013 or a late GAA election was made in years beginning in 2012 for assets placed in service in previous years. A change of accounting method form must be included with the timely-filed income tax return for the year of change, and a copy sent to the IRS in Ogden, Utah. The change number is 197.

A partial disposition election can be made for any asset. Disposition events include a sale, retirement, casualty gain or loss, or tax-deferred exchange.[182] For asset classes 00.11 through 00.4 in Revenue Procedure 87-56, the taxpayer must classify the replacement portion of the asset under the same asset class as the disposed asset.[183]

The election is made by simply reporting the gain or loss or other deduction on the taxpayer's timely-filed original federal income tax return for the taxable year. For asset classes 00.11 through 00.4 in Revenue Procedure 87-56, the taxpayer must also report the

180	REG-110732-13, NPRM REG-110732-13, September 19, 2013.
181	Proposed Treasury Regulations § 1.168(i)-1(e)(2)(i).
182	Proposed Treasury Regulations § 1.168(i)-8(d)(1).
183	Proposed Treasury Regulations § 1.168(i)-8(d)(2).

replacement portion of the asset under the same asset class as the disposed asset.[184]

A taxpayer may use any reasonable method for purposes of determining the unadjusted depreciable basis of the disposed portion at the time of its disposition. An example of a reasonable method includes discounting the original cost of the disposed portion of the asset to its "placed in service year" cost using the Consumer Price Index.[185]

Generally this change can't be made by filing a change of accounting method form.

There is an exception when, in a tax audit, the IRS disallows a deduction for a repair for the replacement of an item for which the partial disposition election wasn't made. In that case, the taxpayer may file for a change of accounting method for that item, provided the taxpayer still owns it at the beginning of the year of change.[186]

The undepreciated cost of the asset is reduced by the disposed portion on the first day of the taxable year in which the disposition occurs. The cost of the disposed portion and its portion of the accumulated depreciation are separately reported and the depreciation stops according to its convention at the time of the disposition.[187]

Remember the cost of the replacement of the partial disposition item must be capitalized as a restoration. See "Improvements that must be capitalized," above.

#

For more information, see IRS Publication 535, Business Expenses. You can get it at www.irs.gov.

184	Proposed Treasury Regulations § 1.168(i)-8(d)(2)(ii)(B).
185	Proposed Treasury Regulations § 1.168(i)-8(e)(3).
186	Proposed Treasury Regulations § 1.168(i)-8(d)(2)(iii).
187	Proposed Treasury Regulations § 1.168(i)-8(h)(3).

11

Family Limited Partnerships (FLPs) - How to Reduce Your Estate Tax For A Family Business Or Real Estate Investments By 35% Or More!

The details of estate planning are beyond the scope of this book. You should seek the help of a qualified team of professionals, including an attorney, life insurance agent, tax advisor, financial planner and others.

With the Tax Cuts and Jobs Act of 2017, estate planning has become more uncertain.

The estate and gift tax exemption has been doubled from $5 million to $10 million, indexed for inflation after 2010, effective for tax years beginning after 2017 and expiring for tax years after 2025. The exemption equivalent for 2020 is $11,580,000. Under the current federal estate tax laws, the estate tax exemption is "portable" for surviving spouses. This means the unused exemption for the last-deceased spouse can be available for the surviving spouse, enabling a married couple to have a combined taxable estate of up to $23,160,000 and not be subject to estate tax.

The exemption increase expires after 2025. The IRS has issued guidance for what will happen after 2025 to exemptions increased using portability elections made by estates of decedents who died before 2026. The exemption for the deceased spouse is not reduced and will be available for the surviving spouse if the surviving spouse qualifies (does not remarry).[188]

For individuals with estates well below the higher exemptions, the emphasis of estate planning has shifted from estate and gift taxes to income taxes. Trusts are now subject to the maximum federal income tax rate of 37% when their taxable income exceeds $12,950. The 3.8% net investment income tax, in addition to the federal income tax, also applies for trusts when their income exceeds $12,950.

The tax basis of certain assets (excluding retirement accounts, which are considered "income with respect of a decedent") that are included in the taxable estate of a decedent are adjusted to fair market value on the date of death, sometimes called a "stepped-up basis," although it could also be "stepped down." Estate plans are being designed to avoid "bypass" strategies and include appreciated family assets in modest estates, including the use of qualified terminable interest property (QTIP) trusts.

Considering the benefit of this "basis step up" and the high exemption amounts, most

---

188   Treasury Regulations § 20.2010-1(c).

taxpayers will find lifetime gifts aren't beneficial.

For those with significant assets, there is a real possibility that future U.S. Presidents and Congresses will decide to cut back the estate tax exemption. Taking maximum advantage of the exemption now available may be worthwhile.

In addition, the various states have different inheritance tax regimes and differences in their laws for transferring property that will require attention from a local attorney.

The benefits of lifetime giving

A number of techniques are available, but it is significant to point out *most of them are based on lifetime gift programs, sometimes including using irrevocable trusts created during your lifetime!* After a person is deceased, the planning opportunities are much more limited. Significantly, gift taxes paid during your lifetime are generally not included in your gross estate. In other words, *you receive an estate tax reduction of up to 40% of the gift taxes you pay for transfers during your lifetime.*

In addition to estate tax benefits, your family may enjoy income tax savings from shifting income to family members in lower income tax brackets.

Caution!

If you need to keep your assets in order to maintain your standard of living and to provide for contingencies such as long-term care, you probably shouldn't pursue an aggressive lifetime giving "wealth preservation" program.

In some cases, receiving significant gifts can corrupt the beneficiaries, eliminating their motivation to work. Don't let the "tax tail" wag the dog! Maybe a charitable giving program makes sense in this situation. (Outright bequests to charities are not subject to estate or gift taxes.)

Family wealth planning using a family partnership or LLC holding real estate

In the situation where the beneficiaries are compatible and have an interest in maintaining the assets of the family, particularly in real estate or a family business, significant estate (and, in some cases, income) tax benefits may be secured using a family business structure. The most popular structures right now are the family limited partnership and the family limited liability company, principally because they permit the donor(s) to retain management control of the assets that are given during his, her, or their life and have significant operational flexibility compared to a corporate structure.

(Note the IRS initiated proposed regulations during 2016 and 2017 to attack family limited partnerships. They have currently abandoned the effort to issue those regulations. They will continue to litigate arrangements that they view as abusive.)

When the donor is willing to give up control, such as letting a younger family member function as a general partner or managing member, it is easier to defend valuation discounts as a "completed gift." The shifting of control supports a business purpose of management succession.

The principle on which the estate tax reduction is based is that a minority interest has a disproportionately lower value than a majority interest in the whole, because of the lack of control of the minority owner and the lack of marketability of a fractional interest in a family partnership. For example, suppose a partnership's business could be sold as a whole for $1,000,000. An investor might only be willing to pay about $150,000 for a 25% interest in the partnership, because he or she would be unable to control the partnership or easily sell the partnership interest. We call the difference between the amount a buyer would pay for a fractional interest (in the example, $150,000) and the proportionate value of the interest based on the whole (in the example, $250,000) a valuation adjustment. Valuation adjustments (reductions) of 35% and up have been defended for partnership interests where there was a lack of control and a lack of marketability.

A donor may make annual fractional gifts to use his or her annual gift exclusion ($15,000 per donor, per donee, per year for 2020) and lifetime gift credit exclusion (equivalent to $11,580,000 of gifts for 2020), thus securing the valuation adjustments for the gifts. If the donor retains less than a 50% interest at his or her death, that interest should also qualify for a valuation adjustment.

There is a significant trade-off for making lifetime transfers. Assets that are included in a decedent's taxable estate receive a "fresh start" tax basis (cost used to compute depreciation, gains and losses) of the fair market value as of the date of death or alternate valuation date. Consult with a tax advisor about this trade-off before going ahead with a lifetime transfer.

Real estate is an ideal asset for a family limited partnership because most of the income is a return on capital, rather than based on individual efforts. This passive characteristic justifies passing through income and deductions to the partners.

Avoid putting personal-use assets, including the donor's residence, in a family limited partnership. Gifts of personal-use assets, unless a fair market value rent is paid for the use of them, are disregarded for estate tax purposes. Also, the sale of a principal residence qualifies for a special tax exclusion (see Chapter 1), so you usually don't want to put it in a family limited partnership or a bypass trust.

Using entity fractionalization for investment assets

Should a family limited partnership or limited liability company be used to hold liquid investments, such as securities, cash and life insurance policies? Such entities may be defended if a legitimate purpose can be established for them, but expect an especially vigorous attack by the IRS. This strategy has been targeted as vulnerable.

The IRS has been more receptive for family limited partnerships and limited liability companies for which the principal assets are investment real estate. In estate tax litigation, families have also been more successful in defending valuation reduction benefits with entities principally holding investment real estate than with entities principally holding liquid investments such as cash and securities.

What the IRS doesn't want you to know

The IRS hates these programs, and has attacked them vigorously. Almost all of the estate tax returns that are currently selected for audit by the IRS have a valuation adjustment. *They have often failed in their efforts, except when the transfers were made shortly before death, the donor didn't retain sufficient assets for his or her support, entity distributions were disproportionately made to the donor for living expenses, and the entity wasn't properly operated.* When the plan is done properly, the IRS will almost always capitulate or make a significant concession in settling the issue.

Properly implementing a family wealth plan is a worthwhile investment

When you are seeking significant tax benefits from this type of plan, it doesn't make sense to "cut corners." A competent attorney should prepare the documents. Valuations should be prepared by a qualified appraiser who is educated in this area. You should use a qualified tax advisor, such as a CPA, to assist in assuring the entity is operated properly, including setting up a separate bank account, setting up separate books and records, properly paying proportionate benefits to partners/members, and preparing income tax returns. The up-front investment will pay dividends to your beneficiaries in tax benefits and avoided litigation costs.

When does entity fractionalization make sense?

As you can see from the above discussion, the entity fractionalization strategy can require a significant investment in professional fees and potential litigation costs. There are three situations where the strategy makes sense. 1) There are assets of significant value to be transferred. ($10 million is worth thinking about.) 2) The assets have a potential for significant growth in value. 3) The assets are generating significant income.

12
Holding Real Estate in an IRA, Roth or Retirement Account

During the real estate boom of the late 1990s and early 2000s, it became popular to look to retirement accounts as sources of funds to buy real estate. The reason is a very practical one – that's where the majority of our assets available to invest are.

You can hold real estate in these retirement accounts. Should you?

Long-term investments in real estate in retirement accounts often aren't tax-favored. For example, rental real estate often generates tax losses from deductions for interest and depreciation. You probably won't be able to use these losses in a retirement account until you sell the property. With the exception of Roth accounts, distributions from retirement accounts are taxable as ordinary income, currently at a 37% maximum federal income tax rate. Compared to when the property is held outside of retirement accounts: assuming the property is held more than one year, most of the gain will probably be taxable at long-term capital gains rates, currently at a 20% maximum federal income tax rate plus a potential 3.8% net investment income tax (see chapter 14).

As I'll explain, income from real estate held in a retirement account can be subject to double taxation – a tax to the retirement account when earned and, again with the exception of a Roth account, a tax to the plan beneficiary when distributions are made.

Alternative real estate-based investments are more tax-favored for retirement accounts than actually holding the real estate. For example, the interest from a "hard money" mortgage is not subject to tax for the retirement account. Another example is buying and selling options to purchase real estate. Although these investments are high risk, they can be used to enhance the returns and build the principal fund of a retirement account.

Roth accounts – special benefit power

Roth accounts have special characteristics that make them especially attractive. Qualified distributions (after a five-year waiting period and after age 59 ½) are tax-free and there are no required minimum distributions during the participant's lifetime. If you meditate on these characteristics, a light bulb should turn on in your head – "Wow!"

The maximum Roth contribution for 2020 is $6,000 plus an additional $1,000 "catch up" contribution for taxpayers who were at least age 50 by the end of the tax year.

A problem is the income levels for phaseout of the Roth contribution. For 2020, the phaseout for single persons is for modified adjusted gross income from $124,000 to $139,000 and $196,000 to $206,000 for married persons who file joint returns. For married persons filing separate returns, the phaseout is modified gross income from $0 to $10,000.

Unlike regular IRA accounts, there is no tax deduction for contributions to a Roth.

Besides regular contributions, there is another way to get a lot more funds into a Roth account – an IRA conversion. After 2009, a $100,000 adjusted gross income limitation was repealed and the conversion became available to all taxpayers.

In some cases, employee retirement accounts (like 401(k) accounts) can be rolled over to IRA accounts as an intermediate step for conversion to a Roth account.

As a result of making the conversion, the amount converted will be subject to current income tax. If you can afford it, the benefits may be significant. The younger you are, the greater the potential benefit of accumulating additional income or appreciation. As you get older (say over age 50), you might want to have an actuarial computation done. People are living longer and longer, so the potential for accumulation keeps increasing. How's your health?

Who will be the trustee/administrator of the plan?

Traditional low-fee retirement account sponsors do not handle accounts with individually-owned real estate investments. Banks and brokerage companies will typically only accept cash, their in-house mutual funds and publicly-traded securities as plan assets. Families of funds that sponsor retirement accounts will usually only offer their own funds as plan asset alternatives.

Companies can set up their own retirement trust accounts that can hold non-traditional assets. These plans could be 401(k), profit sharing, defined benefit or ESOP plans. You need professional help, possibly including an actuary, a lawyer, an accountant and a plan administration company, in setting up these plans. Some larger plans that cover 100 employees or more even required audits by CPA firms. Remember that, as a plan sponsor, you and your company have fiduciary liabilities for managing the plan assets.

There are also self-directed IRA trustees and custodians that charge higher fees for holding these assets.

When you are researching alternatives, you need to ask a lot of questions. Some plans that are called "self-directed" actually permit only limited investments.

Having a self-directed plan can be expensive, time-consuming and a nuisance, especially for company plans. Discuss the details of what is required in your situation with professional advisors before going ahead. You might decide it's not worth it.

Unrelated business income

Many people aren't aware that "tax exempt" entities, including charities and retirement plans, are subject to income taxes on certain types of income, called "unrelated business income."[189] How to apply the tax rules for unrelated business income is one of the more

189   IRC § 408(e)(1), §408A(a) and § 511(a)(2).

complex sections of the income tax laws.

The federal tax form on which the income tax is computed for tax-exempt entities is Form 990-T, Exempt Organization Income Tax Return. You can get a copy of the form and instructions at the IRS web site, www.irs.gov.

When tax-exempt trusts, like retirement accounts, are subject to the tax on unrelated business income, they are generally taxed under the rules and rates that apply to trusts.[190] The first $1,000 of unrelated business income is not subject to tax. For 2020, taxable income over $12,950 is subject to the 37% maximum federal income tax rate.

For example, when properties are bought and sold in "quick turn" or "flip" transactions, these transactions may be determined to be a trade or business.[191] The properties are not considered to be held for investment, but for sale to customers in the ordinary course of a trade or business. These transactions and related business expenses should be reported as unrelated business income.

The IRS has "looked through" an IRA to find a "wash sale" for a sale of securities by the participant and purchase by the IRA. This may be an indication the IRS could try to aggregate "quick sale" transactions in multiple IRA accounts to find a trade or business, resulting in unrelated business income.[192]

There is a special exception for property purchased by a tax exempt entity from a financial institution in conservatorship or receivership or from the conservator or receiver of such a financial institution. The property must have been identified within the 9-month period beginning on the date of its acquisition as property held for sale, but *no more than one-half* of property acquired in a single transaction may be designated. The sale must take place before the later of (1) the date 30 months after the date of acquisition of the property, or (2) a date otherwise specified by the IRS. While the property was held by the tax exempt entity, the total expenditures on improvements and development activities included in the basis of the property may not exceed 20% of the net selling price of the property.[193]

Trade or business income of a partnership or an S corporation for which the tax-exempt entity has an ownership interest is unrelated business income.[194] There is a special exception for S corporation employer shares held by an ESOP.[195]

Any income received from a "controlled entity," including rental income which would not usually be subject to tax, is taxed as net unrelated trade or business income.[196]

190	IRC § 511(b)(2).
191	IRC § 512(b)(5)(b) and § 513(a).
192	Revenue Ruling 2008-5.
193	IRC § 8512(b)(16).
194	IRC § 512(c) and § 512(e).
195	IRC § 512(e)(3).
196	IRC § 512(b)(13).

The general rule is rental income from rental real estate is not unrelated business income,[197] but see below about debt-financed income. Rent from personal property that is incidental to renting real estate is also not unrelated business income. To be "incidental," the rent for the personal property may not exceed 10% of the total rents for all property leased.

Gains from the sale of real estate are also generally not unrelated business income, unless the property is inventory or held for sale to customers for a trade or business, or the gain is debt-financed income.[198]

Unrelated debt-financed income.

Real estate is an especially attractive investment vehicle because you can use leverage to enhance your returns. This means you can finance a big portion of the purchase price and control a big value of property with a relatively small cash investment.

When you use leverage to purchase property in an IRA or Roth, a proportionate part of the income, including rental income and gain when the property is sold, is unrelated business taxable income. A percentage (an average of the acquisition indebtedness divided by the average adjusted basis of the property during the period it's held by the organization during the taxable year) [199] is applied to the income and deductions to compute the amounts to be reported on the unrelated business tax return.

There is a special exception from the unrelated debt-financed income rule for company retirement accounts, including 401(k)s, profit-sharing plans and pension plans (but not Simplified Employee Pensions (SEPs)) and government retirement accounts.[200]

Prohibited transactions

Retirement accounts, including IRAs and Roths, are subject to restrictions relating to certain transactions they can participate in. These are called "prohibited transactions."

The consequences for IRAs and Roths when the participant engages in prohibited transactions are particularly severe. The account loses its tax exemption and all of the assets of the account are considered distributed.[201]

Other retirement accounts pay an initial penalty of 15% of the amount involved, and the penalty increases to 100% if the transaction isn't corrected "within the taxable period."[202]

For example, the sale or exchange, or leasing, of any property between a plan and a

---

197	IRC § 512(b)(3).
198	IRC § 512(b)(5).
199	IRC § 512(a).
200	IRC § 514(c)(9).
201	IRC § 408(e)(2), § 408A(a), and 4975(c)(3).
202	IRC § 4975 (b).

disqualified person is a prohibited transaction.[203]

An IRA owner is a "disqualified person" as a "fiduciary."[204] A "fiduciary" includes any person who exercises any discretionary authority or discretionary control respecting management of the plan or exercises any authority or control respecting management or disposition of its assets.[205] The IRS has said that the mere ability to select what company will hold the IRA account is sufficient to be a fiduciary.[206]

The spouse, ancestor, lineal descendant and any spouse of a lineal descendant of a fiduciary are also disqualified persons.[207]

This means an IRA or Roth owner can't buy a property from an IRA without getting a waiver from the IRS.[208] The only way to take a property out for personal use is for the plan to distribute the property. For accounts other than Roth accounts, the fair market value of the property would be ordinary taxable income to the plan beneficiary when received. Distributions to a beneficiary before age 59 ½ may also be subject to a penalty for early distributions.

The IRA can't rent a property to the owner's children or parents, but can rent a property to the owner's brother, sister or cousin.

The IRA owner should avoid handling currency relating to real estate owned by an IRA, such as receiving cash rent payments or handling petty cash funds. I recommend using an independent property manager to handle the transactions.

Valuation concerns

Minimum distributions are required to be made from an IRA when the IRA is an inherited account and when a participant-owner reaches age 72. In order to compute the required minimum distribution, the fair market value (FMV) at the beginning of the year must be known.

The IRA custodian should report the fair market value of the assets held in the account as of December 31 of the year. The IRS has issued instructions for Form 5498 stating that the FMV for certain specified assets should be reported together with codes for the related assets. One of the specified assets is real estate.

The IRS has not specified how these assets should be valued. If appraisals are required, the cost of maintaining self-directed retirement accounts could increase dramatically, possibly prohibitively.

---

203   IRC § 4975(c)(1)(A).
204   IRC § 4975((e)(2)(A).
205   IRC § 4975(e)(3)(A).
206   Letter Ruling 200324018, 2/24/2003.
207   IRC §§ 4975(e)(2)(F) and 4975(e)(6).
208   IRC § 4975(c)(2).

I asked a representative for the custodian industry who will be responsible for getting the valuation amounts. The response was the custodian will report amounts provided by the account owner. If the account owner can't provide the information, the custodian will resign from the account.

#

For additional information, see IRS Publication 498, "Tax on Unrelated Business Income of Exempt Organizations," IRS Publication 560, "Retirement Plans For Small Business," and IRS Publication 590, "Individual Retirement Arrangements." Also see Form 5498 and the related instructions. You can get copies at www.irs.gov.

Also, see my book, *How To Use Roth & IRA Accounts To Provide A Secure Retirement, 2020 Edition.* It will be available at Amazon, BN.com, and as an ebook for Kindle and the Nook at Amazon, BN.com and the Apple Store on December 1, 2020.

13
Materials and Supplies

Certain low-cost items are allowed to be currently deducted, even though they may last more than one year. The rules under which they are deductible are called the "de minimis rules." In addition, rules are defined for materials and supplies.

Regulations relating to capitalization and repairs were issued by the IRS on September 13, 2013.[209] See chapter 10. These regulations are optionally effective earlier, but generally effective starting in 2014. The regulations include de minimis rules, which weren't previously defined or available except at the discretion of an IRS agent.

Materials and supplies

Non-incidental materials and supplies are generally deductible in the taxable year in which the materials and supplies are first used in the taxpayer's operations or are consumed in the taxpayer's operations.[210] If a cash basis taxpayer purchases the item and immediately uses it, it's currently tax deductible.

Amounts paid to acquire or produce incidental materials and supplies that are carried on hand and for which no record of consumption is kept or for which physical inventories at the beginning and end of the taxable year are not taken are deductible in the taxable year in which the amounts are paid, provided taxable income is clearly reflected.[211]

Materials and supplies are tangible property that is used or consumed in the taxpayer's operations that is not inventory and that:

(i) is a component acquired to maintain, repair or improve a unit of tangible property owned, leased or serviced by the taxpayer and that is not acquired as part of any single unit of tangible property;

(ii) consists of fuel, lubricants, water, and similar items, reasonably expected to be consumed in 12 months or less, beginning when used in the taxpayer's operations;

(iii) is a unit of property that has an economic useful life of 12 months or less, beginning when the property is used or consumed in the taxpayer's operations;

(iv) is a unit of property that has an acquisition cost or production cost of $200 or less (or other amount later specified in published guidance by the IRS); or

---

209   T.D. 9636.
210   Treasury Regulations § 1.162-3(a)(1).
211   Treasury Regulations § 1.162-3(a)(2).

(v)   is otherwise identified in published guidance by the IRS.[212]

Therefore, most supply items that cost $200 or less are currently deductible.

Standby emergency spare parts

Standby emergency spare parts are considered to be materials and supplies to which the $200 limitation and the $5,000 or $2,500 de minimis elections apply.

Standby emergency parts are items set aside for use as replacements to avoid substantial operational time loss caused by emergencies due to particular machinery or equipment failure. They are not interchangeable in other machines and equipment. They are not acquired in quantity (generally only one is on hand for each piece of machinery or equipment). They are not repaired and reused.[213]

Rotable and spare parts

There are complex rules defined for rotable and spare parts that are beyond the scope of this discussion. I don't expect them to apply for most real estate operations. Discuss with a qualified tax advisor whether they apply to you.

De Minimis with an applicable financial statement

The most liberal de minimis rule allowing the deduction of low cost items applies to taxpayers with an applicable financial statement. In most cases for real estate projects, that means the entity will have financial statements that are audited by an independent CPA firm.

The financial statements must be used for a nontax purpose, such as:
1)   credit purposes;
2)   reporting to shareholders, partners, or similar persons;
3)   any other substantial non-tax purpose; or
4)   a financial statement (not a tax return) required to be provided to the federal or a state government or any federal or state agency (other than the SEC or the IRS).

Just distribute the audited financial statements to the shareholders or owners and give them to your banker. Otherwise, why bother with the expense and inconvenience to have an audit done?

If the taxpayer adopts the accounting procedure and makes the proper election as explained below, items that cost up to $5,000 per invoice, or per item as substantiated by the invoice, can be currently deducted.[214] The IRS may specify other amounts in published guidance.

---

212   Treasury Regulations §1.162-3(c)(1).
213   Treasury Regulations §1.162-3(c)(2).
214   Treasury Regulations §1.263(a)-1(f)(i)(B).

For example, a taxpayer could buy 5 personal computers for $3,000 each and deduct the entire $15,000 cost.

In order to claim the deduction, the taxpayer must also have (at the beginning of the taxable year) written accounting procedures treating as an expense for non-tax purposes: (1) amounts paid for property costing less than the specified dollar amount (currently $5,000), or (2) amounts paid for property with an economic useful life of 12 months or less.

(Although the "economic useful life of 12 months or less" statement is required, the IRS gives an example that makes it clear the dollar limitation controls.[215] If the "economic useful life of 12 months or less" applies but the cost exceeds the thresholds, the taxpayer should expense the item on its books and records but capitalize it on its income tax return, resulting in an accounting difference for this item. Considering the IRS was trying to encourage conformity of a taxpayer's accounting records and tax reporting, it's unfortunate they adopted this rule.)

The taxpayer must also follow the written procedure and expense these amounts on its applicable financial statement.

The election will also have to be made each year on a statement attached to the taxpayer's timely filed income tax return.

There is an anti-abuse rule for if the taxpayer tries to use the election to manipulate its tax liability. Also, if the cost for an item is "componentized" onto separate invoices, they will be aggregated. For example, if the cost of a car is separately stated as for tires, engine and body, they will be added together for the total cost of the car.

Standard charges for an item included on the invoice such as for delivery, installation, and sales tax are included in the total cost. They may be allocated to several items on an invoice on a reasonable basis. If the delivery or installation charges are on a separate invoice, they don't have to be added to the total cost.

As you can see, there are a number of "hoops" to go through, including adopting the required accounting procedure before the beginning of the taxable year, that can create problems for some taxpayers.

Since it is an annual election, the de minimis rule is not an accounting procedure for which Form 3115, Change of Accounting Procedure, is required.

De Minimis rule with no applicable financial statement

Most real estate investors won't have an applicable financial statement.

---

215   Treasury Regulations § 1.263-1(f)(7), Example 8.

The rules are very similar to those for taxpayers with an applicable financial statement, but, effective for tax years beginning after 2016, the limit per invoice or item on an invoice is $2,500 instead of $5,000.

These taxpayers will have to be diligent in adopting the accounting procedure and following it in their recordkeeping. Although the election isn't required to be in writing, it's best to do so in order to document that it was in place as of the beginning of the year. The people who keep records for these taxpayers often aren't professional accountants. Even bookkeepers who work for CPA firms could mess this up.

Whoever prepares the income tax returns will have to remember to include an annual de minimis election.

The lower $2,500 threshold means deducting five $3,000 computers, like in the "applicable financial statement" example, is out. How about a $250 tablet computer, a $250 printer, a $100 calculator and a $500 smart phone? Yes!

Remember that items that can't be deducted under the $200 general limitation or the $500 de minimis rule can be alternatively expensed under Internal Revenue Code Section 179.

Also remember every item that meets the requirements must be consistently expensed to apply the de minimis rule. No exceptions allowed!

Some items must still be capitalized

The Internal Revenue Code includes Uniform Capitalization Rules under which costs must be capitalized even if they would otherwise be deductible under the exceptions above.

For example, materials and supplies consumed in producing inventory items to be resold must be capitalized.

Another example relating to real estate is if materials and supplies are consumed as part of a remodeling or rehabilitation project, they must be capitalized.

14
Net Investment Income Tax

Congress enacted the 3.8% Net Investment Income (NII) tax as part of the Health Care Reform legislation or Patient Protection and Affordable Care Act of 2010 (ACA), commonly called Obamacare. The popular parts of that legislation became effective early, such as extending parent's health care coverage to adult children under age 27. The less popular parts, such as penalties for not having health care, mandated health care for large employers and the NII tax, had delayed effective dates.

The NII tax first became effective in 2013.

The rationale for the 3.8% rate is a replacement for Medicare tax revenue on investment income that would otherwise apply to wages and self-employment income of high-income individuals. The taxes collected don't go to Medicare or health care, but to the general fund.

The NII tax is very complex and represents a new chapter in the Internal Revenue Code, but it borrows and piggybacks many existing tax rules. Although Form 8960 is only one page, the instructions are 20 pages and my printout of the regulations is 98 pages. The closest parallel significant development that I can come up with is the adoption of the alternative minimum tax.

Although the NII tax was enacted in 2010, the IRS didn't issue final regulations for the tax until November 26, 2013. (The final regulations are effective for tax years beginning after December 31, 2013.) Remember the constitutionality of the Health Care Reform package was being litigated and many believed the Supreme Court would rule against the tax. The Supreme Court ruled in favor of the Health Care Reform package on June 28, 2012. It seems to me the IRS was either hoping the whole problem would go away, or "waiting to cross the bridge until they came to it."

Legal challenge to the Net Investment Income Tax

The U. S. Supreme Court has agreed to hear *California v. Texas* (U.S. Supreme Court Docket 19-840) addressing the constitutionality of the ACA after the Tax Cuts and Jobs Act of 2017 eliminated the penalty for failing to have health insurance. If the Supreme Court finds the ACA is unconstitutional, the NII tax could also be eliminated. Taxpayers who previously paid the NII tax can file protective claims for refund that would be effective if the Supreme Court finds the NII tax is unconstitutional. The deadline for filing a protective claim for taxes paid on timely filed 2016 federal income tax returns was July 15, 2020. If the 2016 federal income tax return was filed on extension, the due date for the protective claim for 2016 is October 15, 2020. See your tax advisor for later tax years.

An amended income tax return is not required for a protective refund claim. The protective claim should be sent to the mailing address where the taxpayer would send Form 1040X. The claim must be in writing and signed. Here are the items to include:

- The taxpayer's name, address, Social Security Number or ITIN, and other contact information;
- A description of the contingencies the claim is based on (the pending outcome of *California v. Texas*);
- The essential nature of the claim (the refund of the 0.9% additional Medicare tax and the 3.8% net investment income tax); and
- The specific year(s) for which a refund is sought.[216]

Whole books are going to be devoted to the NII tax. I am just going to hit some highlights here and focus on its interplay with real estate and the passive activity rules. The passive activity rules are explained as they relate to losses in Chapter 8.

How do you compute the NII tax?

The NII tax applies for married taxpayers who file joint returns with modified adjusted gross income over $250,000, married filing separate returns with modified AGI over $125,000, and singles with modified adjusted gross income over $200,000. Note these thresholds aren't indexed for inflation. It also applies to U.S. estates and trusts, with income subject to the maximum tax rate, $12,950 for 2020. The threshold for estates and trusts is indexed for inflation. Tax-exempt trusts, including retirement accounts and charitable remainder trusts, aren't subject to the tax. Nonresident aliens aren't subject to the tax.

Trusts are being clobbered by this tax together with being subject to the 37% maximum federal tax rate at a low threshold and require special attention to planning distributions.

To compute modified adjusted gross income, start with adjusted gross income on page one of your income tax return, then add the exclusion from income that applies to U.S. citizens or permanent residents who work overseas.

The tax is 3.8% of the lesser of net investment income or the excess of modified adjusted gross income over the threshold. For example, Sally is a single person with modified adjusted gross income of $250,000 and net investment income of $25,000. Her tax would be 3.8% of $25,000, or $950. Note that the amount she pays to determine that tax might be more than the tax.

Although the tax will be reported on your individual income tax return, it is a separate tax. Regular tax credits, such as the minimum tax credit and the research credit, can't be used to reduce the NII tax.

---

216   *Spidell's Flash E-mail*: "Additional ACA protective claim guidance", July 14, 2020.

What is net investment income?

There are three categories of investment income, and taxpayers subject to the tax will be required to identify the amounts for each category.

(1) Income from interest, dividends, annuities, royalties, and rents, other than such income derived from an active trade or business.

(2) A passive trade or business for which the income isn't subject to self-employment tax.

(3) Net gain attributable to the disposition of property, other than property held in an active trade or business.

You get to subtract from investment income deductions attributable to that income, including state income taxes attributable to the income.

Passive activities, real estate professionals and the NII tax

Passive activities have become even more significant with the adoption of the NII tax. (See Chapter 8 for the passive activity rules relating to loss limitations.)

In the past, passive activities were only significant if you had losses. Passive activity losses are generally limited to passive activity income. Any excess is carried over until the activity is sold, abandoned or liquidated. Effective for tax years beginning after 2017, "excess business losses" are also suspended and added to a taxpayer's net operating loss carryover. See Chapter 8.

Suddenly whether an activity is passive is also important when it is profitable and the owner has significant income. Note under item (2) above that income from passive activities is investment income.

Also notice that income subject to self-employment tax isn't subject to the NII tax. The reason is the NII tax was rationalized as a substitute for the Medicare tax, which applies to self-employment income.

Net income from the rental of real estate is a unique form of business income because it is statutorily excluded from the self-employment tax. If we can make it non-passive, it isn't subject to either the self-employment tax or the NII tax. Cool!

Under (1) above, rental income is investment income unless it is trade or business income. The final regulations include a safe harbor for a qualifying real estate professional who participates in one or more real estate activities for more than 500 hours during a taxable year or has participated in those activities or more than 500 hours in any five taxable years during the ten tax years immediately preceding the taxable year. The net income from the rental real estate that meets these requirements is not subject to the net investment income tax.[217]

---

217   Treasury Regulations § 1.1411-4(g)(7).

Qualifying as a real estate professional is not a "slam dunk." See Chapter 8. The IRS is already successfully challenging real estate professional status for loss limitations. The new NII tax will lead to even more litigation.

Gains and losses

I think a common error in self-prepared income tax returns will be missing the exclusion of gains and losses from the disposition of assets used in a non-passive trade or business from the net investment income tax. This would include gains and losses from the disposition of assets in a rental real estate activity that a taxpayer has claimed is non-passive under the real estate professional rules.[218]

The default in most software will probably be to carry gains and losses from the disposition of property to net investment income. There will probably be codes to enter to classify the gains as not investment income. The preparer will have to remember to include the input to exclude these gains from NII.

The IRS has issued complex guidelines for how dispositions of passthrough interests such as partnerships, LLCs and S corporations should be treated. Part of the gain may be allocable to the disposition of trade or business assets and not investment income and part may be attributable to the investment in the entity and reported as investment income. The devil is in the details of figuring how much goes in each category, because businesses can consist of thousands of assets.

Tax planning strategies for the NII tax

Aside from qualifying as a real estate professional and electing to aggregate your properties as a single activity, other traditional real estate strategies can help defer or eliminate the NII tax. If a married couple can keep their modified adjusted gross income under $250,000 or minimize the excess over that amount, they might have no NII tax or a very small amount. (Remember it's 3.8%, not the end of the world.)

For example, an installment sale can be used to spread taxable gain over several years. (Chapter 4.)

A tax-deferred exchange can be used to avoid current taxation of a capital gain until the replacement property is sold, possibly leading to another exchange. (Chapter 5.)

Depreciation can be used to shelter rental income from current taxation. (Chapter 7.)

Investments made and accumulated in an individual retirement account or a qualified retirement plan are not subject to the NII tax. Distributions received from these accounts also aren't subject to the NII tax. (Chapter 12.)

Choosing an appropriate entity for conducting your real estate business can make a difference in whether self-employment tax or NII tax may apply. (Chapter 6.)

---

218   Treasury Regulations § 1.1411-4(c)(4).

Another strategy not discussed at length in this book is participating in a nonqualified deferred compensation plan at work. By deferring receiving compensation income until after retirement, the income may be taxed in a lower marginal tax bracket and you might be able to keep your modified adjusted gross income below the threshold for NII tax.

Get professional help

With the adoption of the NII tax, it appears to me that high-income taxpayers who don't seek professional help with tax planning and tax return preparation are crazy.

#

For additional information, see Form 8960, Net Investment Income Tax – Individuals, Estates and Trusts and instructions at the IRS web site, www.irs.gov.

15

The Deduction For Noncorporate Business Income (Passthrough Deduction)

The Tax Cuts and Jobs Act of 2017 includes a 20% tax deduction for "pass-through business income."[219] The deduction is effective for tax years beginning after December 31, 2017 and expires after December 31, 2025. It is extraordinarily complex.

Books will be written about this deduction. The IRS has issued proposed and final regulations to clarify many issues.[220] The final regulations are effective for tax years ending after February 8, 2019, and can optionally be applied for earlier tax years (2018 for calendar year taxpayers). Taxpayers may alternatively rely on the proposed regulations for 2018.

My printout of the final regulations and explanation is 246 pages. I can only give a sketchy explanation here. Although tax return preparation software includes features to compute the deduction, business owners should really hire a professional tax return preparer who is familiar with the rules to assure the deduction is properly computed.

Here are some differences between the proposed regulations and the final regulations.

(1) The final regulations specify these items must be subtracted when computing Qualified Business Income:

- The deduction for self-employment tax;
- the self-employed health insurance deduction; and
- the deduction for qualified retirement plan contributions.

(2) The final regulations allow passthrough entities to elect to aggregate activities.

There are elements of the 20% of QBI deduction for which tax planning can be done to get a better result, so it will be worthwhile to discuss the deduction with your tax advisor.

---

219   Internal Revenue Code Section 199A.
220   Proposed Treasury Regulations REG-107892-18, published August 16, 2018, and Final Treasury Regulations REG-107892-18, published February 8, 2019.

Which taxpayers are eligible

The deduction can apply when the taxpayer is a sole proprietor (including owning rental real estate) or an owner of an S corporation, real estate investment trust, partnership, or LLC taxed as a partnership or sole proprietorship.

A new deduction category

This is a new deduction category, after computing adjusted gross income but before itemized deductions or the standard deduction.

How do you compute the deduction?

The deduction is the lesser of (1) the "combined qualified business income amount" of the taxpayer, or (2) 20% of the excess, if any, of the taxable income of the taxpayer for the tax year over the net capital gain for the tax year.

The "combined qualified business income amount" for a tax year is (1) the deductible amount for each qualified trade or business of the taxpayer, PLUS (2) 20% of the aggregate amount of qualified real estate investment trust dividends and qualified publicly traded partnership income of the taxpayer.

The deductible amount for each qualified trade or business is the lesser of (1) 20% of the taxpayer's qualified business income for the trade or business, or (2) the greater of (i) 50% of the W-2 wages for the trade or business or (ii) the sum of 25% of the business's W-2 wages plus 2.5% of the unadjusted basis (cost before depreciation) of all qualified property as of the end of the taxable year. (The unadjusted basis of qualified property is reduced by any amount expensed under Internal Revenue Code Section 179. Bonus depreciation will usually be more advantageous for computing the deduction for noncorporate business income. The unadjusted basis of qualified property is only included in the computation for the greater of (1) 10 years after the property is placed in service or (2) the life for the modified cost recovery system after the property is placed in service (27.5 years for residential real estate and 39 years for commercial real estate.))

So a business that leases all of its equipment and real estate and uses contract labor would not receive a tax deduction.

A sole proprietor consultant with no employees and little equipment would receive a very small tax deduction.

The limitation for renting residential real estate that is a trade or business will usually be computed as 2.5% of the depreciable basis of the residence.

Qualified business income includes items of income, gain, deduction and loss to the extent those items are effectively connected with the conduct of a trade or business within the United States. Any amount less than zero is treated as qualified business loss for the next tax year. Qualified business income does not include investment income, reasonable compensation paid by a qualified trade or business, or guaranteed payments to a partner or

LLC owner for services to the business.

(Note that if an S corporation, the IRS can recharacterize part of the allocated income of the owner to compensation, which won't qualify for the deduction. The IRS can't do this for a partnership or a sole proprietorship.)

Does rental real estate income qualify?

Will rental real estate income qualify as "trade or business" income for the deduction? It's evident from a limitation of the deduction being computed based on the undepreciated tax basis of depreciable assets that Congress did intend for some rental real estate activities to qualify. Also, certain income from real estate investment trusts qualifies, so why not other rental real estate activities? Some rental real estate arrangements, such as triple-net leases where the owner has no maintenance responsibilities, can be viewed as investments, somewhat like a bond, and will not be treated as a "trade or business" for computing the deduction for noncorporate business income. (If a taxpayer is treating a rental real estate activity as a "trade or business" for this deduction, the taxpayer should issue 1099s for service payments of $600 or more to attorneys and noncorporate services providers, and for interest payments.)

Safe harbor for rental real estate.

The IRS has issued a safe-harbor for rental real estate to be treated as a trade or business for the 20% deduction for Qualified Business Income.[221] The safe-harbor is effective for taxable years ending after December 31, 2017. In the notice, the IRS states that rental real estate that doesn't meet the safe-harbor requirements can still qualify as a trade or business. Commercial and residential real estate may not be part of the same enterprise. The requirements for the safe harbor are:

(A) Separate books and records are maintained to reflect income and expenses for each rental real estate enterprise;

(B) For tax years beginning before January 1, 2023, 250 or more hours of rental services are performed per year with respect to the rental enterprise. For tax years beginning after December 31, 2022, the 250-hour test can be met for any three of the five consecutive tax years that end with the tax year.

(C) The taxpayer maintains contemporaneous records, including time reports, logs, or similar documents, regarding: (i) hours of all services performed; (ii) description of all services performed; (iii) dates on which the services were performed; and (iv) who performed the services. The contemporaneous records requirement doesn't apply to the taxable year beginning before January 1, 2019.

---

221   Revenue Procedure 2019-38 superseded Treasury Notice 2019-07.

Rental services include (i) advertising to rent or lease the real estate; (ii) negotiating and executing leases; (iii) verifying information contained in prospective tenant applications; (iv) collection of rent; (v) daily operation, maintenance, and repair of the property; (vi) management of the real estate; (vii) purchase of materials; and (viii) supervision of employees and independent contractors.

Rental services may be performed by owners or by employees, agents, and/or independent contractors of the owners. Rental services do not include financial or investment management activities, like arranging financing; procuring property; studying and reviewing financial statements or reports on operations; planning, managing or constructing long-term capital improvements; or *hours spent traveling to and from the real estate*.

It might be practically impossible to get hourly accounting records from independent contractors.

The following arrangements are not eligible for the safe harbor:

1. Real estate used by the taxpayer or certain related parties as a residence under Section 280A (principal residence for exclusion of gain (see Chapter 1)).

2. Real estate rented under a triple net lease. A triple net lease includes a lease agreement that requires the tenant or lessee to pay taxes, fees and insurance, and to be responsible for maintenance activities of the property in addition to rent and utilities.

3. Real estate rented to a trade or business conducted by a taxpayer or a passthrough entity which is commonly controlled is not eligible for the safe harbor.

4. Real estate for which any portion is rented to a specified service trade or business.

Taxpayers may elect to treat similar commercial properties or residential properties as a single rental real estate enterprise under the safe harbor. Mixed-use properties may not be combined with other properties. Once the election is made, the properties must continue to be combined in later tax years. The books and records may be kept for the combined properties treated as a single enterprise or separate records may be kept for each property and then consolidated.

In order to qualify for the safe harbor, the taxpayer or passthrough entity must include a statement attached to the return on which it claims the Section 199A deduction or passes through Section 199A information that the safe harbor requirements have been satisfied. Under the original Treasury Notice, the statement was required to be signed by the taxpayer or an authorized representative of an eligible taxpayer or passthrough entity. The signature requirement was eliminated by the Revenue Procedure.

What if you don't elect the safe harbor?

Real estate might still qualify as a trade or business when it doesn't meet the safe harbor. Outside the Second Circuit Court of Appeals (outside Connecticut, New York and Vermont), the Tax Court follows fairly liberal rules to classify rental real estate as a trade or business, mostly based on who is responsible for the maintenance of the property.[222]

The standard for a trade or business in the Second Circuit Court of Appeals revolves around "regular and continuous management activity." A single residential rental unit usually won't qualify as a trade or business in the Second Circuit.[223]

When it has served its own purpose, the IRS has asserted rental real estate is a trade or business. Currently, considering the Net Investment Income Tax and the 20% deduction for Qualified Business Income, it is leaning to saying rental real estate is NOT a trade or business.

Does claiming rental real estate as a trade or business give you a tax benefit?

Since most rental real estate operations generate losses subject to the passive activity loss limitations and long-term gains from rental real estate aren't eligible for the 20% deduction, it might favor the taxpayer to "go with the flow" and report rental real estate as not a trade or business. When the activity is sold, suspended passive activity losses of a trade or business will reduce Qualified Business Income, reducing the 20% deduction. Also consider the interplay with the Net Investment Income tax. Long-term gains from the sale of trade or business property aren't subject to the net investment income tax.

Specified service businesses

The deduction does not apply to specified service businesses, but it does apply to engineering and architectural businesses. A specified service trade or business is a trade or business performing services in the fields of health, law, consulting, athletics, financial services, brokerage services, or any trade or business where the principal asset of the trade or business is the reputation or skill of one or more of the employees or owners, or which involves the performance of services that consist of investing and investment management trading, or dealing in securities, partnership interests or commodities. The disqualification of income for specified service businesses doesn't apply when a married couple has taxable income of up to $326,600 and other taxpayers have taxable income up to $163,300 for 2020. These thresholds are indexed for inflation. The deduction is phased out for the taxpayers over these thresholds for the next $100,000 of taxable income for married persons filing joint returns and $50,000 for other taxpayers.

---

222   *Hazard v. Commissioner*, 7 TC 372, 1946, acq. 1946-2 CB 3. This analysis is based on research done by Gary R. McBride, CPA, LLM. *Real Estate Taxation*, 4th Quarter, 2015, p. 16 "Rental Real Estate Trade or Business—The NIIT and Beyond" and *Real Estate Taxation*, 2nd Quarter, 2016, "Rental Real Estate Trade or Business—The NIIT and Beyond, Part II."

223   *Grier v. U.S.*, 218 Fd. 2d 603, Second Circuit, 1955.

(Some married taxpayers might find it's advantageous to file separate tax returns when applying the taxable income limitation. That usually won't be the case in community property states, like California, because one-half of business income will usually be allocated to each spouse.)

The business of being an employee

The deduction does not apply to "the business of being an employee."

Aggregation of businesses

A key consideration of the final regulations is aggregation or combining the income, deductions, wages and property of more than one trade or business. Remember a limitation of the 20% deduction for QBI is the greater of (i) 50% of the W-2 wages paid, or (ii) 25% of the W-2 wages paid and 2.5% of the basis before accumulated depreciation of qualified property attributable to a trade or business. A business with no wages or depreciable property doesn't qualify for a deduction.

Once an individual chooses to aggregate two or more trades or businesses, the individual must consistently report the aggregated trades or businesses in all subsequent tax years. (Individuals were allowed to file an amended income tax return for 2018 to make the aggregation election for that year.) An individual may add a newly-created or newly acquired trade or business to a previously aggregated group. If there is a significant change in facts or circumstances such that the aggregated group no longer qualifies, the individual must redetermine a new permissible aggregation, if any.

Six conditions must be met for trades and businesses to be aggregated.

(1) The activity must be a trade or business, not a hobby or an investment, owned directly or through a passthrough entity.

(2) 50% or more common ownership. Family attribution of brothers, sisters, spouse, ancestors and lineal descendants and attribution of a fiduciary of a trust and a beneficiary of the trust applies to determine common ownership.

(3) The common ownership standard must be met both (a) for the majority of the tax year and (b) on the last day of the tax year.

(4) The trades or businesses must have the same tax years, and short years are ignored.

(5) Specified service trades or businesses (professions excluding engineering and architecture) aren't eligible for aggregation.

(6) Must meet two of three business integration factors.

(a) Same products, property or services.

(b) Shared facilities or centralized business elements.

(c) Coordination or reliance on one another.

The proposed regulations didn't allow passthrough entities to aggregate activities. The details are passed through for the owners to make their own aggregation elections. The final regulations allow passthrough entities to aggregate activities in addition to allowing the owners to make their own aggregation elections.

Which wages are used for the limitation?

Note that wages for computing the limitation for the 20% of QBI deduction might be different from the wages deducted on the income tax return. It will usually be the total of the amounts reported on Forms W-2 for all of the employees for the calendar year ending during the individual's or passthrough entity's taxable year.[224] Wages that are paid by a third party payer are also counted based on the amounts reported on Form W-2 and the third party payers can't include those wages when computing their own 20% of QBI deduction.[225]

For additional information, see Forms 8995-A, Qualified Business Income Deduction and 8995, Qualified Business Income Deduction Simplified Computation and instructions at the IRS web site, www.irs.gov.

---

224   Treasury Regulations § 1.199A-2(b)(2)(i).
225   Treasury Regulations § 1.199A-2(b)(2)(ii).

16

Qualified Opportunity Zones – A New Opportunity To Defer or Avoid Federal Income Tax on Capital Gains

Capital gains deferral for up to eight years? Tax-free investment growth? Sounds too good to be true?

The Tax Cuts and Jobs Act of 2017, enacted on December 22, 2017 and mostly effective for individuals for 2018 through 2026, includes a significant tax benefit – investing in Qualified Opportunity Zones.[226]

This new kind of investment got a slow start because it is tax sensitive and the investment community had to wait for guidelines from the IRS to find out how they can safely operate. Proposed Treasury Regulations were published on May 1, 2019[227] and Final Treasury Regulations were published on January 13, 2020.[228]

The final Treasury Regulations are effective for tax years beginning after March 13, 2020. Taxpayers may choose to apply the final regulations or the proposed regulations for 2018 or 2019, but must apply them consistently.[229]

My printout of the final regulations and IRS explanation is 544 pages. I can only hit some highlights here.

A summary of tax benefits

Here is a summary of the tax benefits:

1. Effective January 1, 2018 through December 31, 2026, if an individual reinvests short- or long-term capital gains from a transaction with an unrelated party within 180 days after a start date in Qualified Opportunity Zone (QOZ) property, the reinvested gain won't be subject to current taxation, but will be deferred until the earlier of the date the QOZ property is sold or liquidated, or December 31, 2026. When it is taxed on the "inclusion date" or December 31, 2026, the gain will retain its character as short-term or long-term capital gain.

2. If the investment is held for at least five years, the potential tax on 10% of the

---

226   Internal Revenue Code Section 1400Z.
227   REG-120186-18.
228   TD 9889.
229   Treasury Regulations § 1.1400Z2(g).

reinvested gain will be forgiven by a basis adjustment to the QOZ property. (Capital gains for property sold after 2020 probably won't qualify for this exclusion.)

3. If the investment is held for at least seven years, the potential tax on 5% of the reinvested Bain will be forgiven by a basis adjustment to the QOZ property. (Capital gains for property sold after 2018 probably won't qualify for this exclusion.)

4. This means that, provided the holding period requirements are met and the property is held through December 31, 2026, 85% of the reinvested gain will be taxable on December 31, 2026.

5. If the QOZ property is held for at least 10 years and the taxpayer makes an election to do so, any additional gain from the ultimate sale or liquidation of the property will be *tax free!*

How the election is made

Taxpayers must elect on their federal income tax returns to defer gain reinvested in QOZ property.[230] The election is made on Form 8949, with Code Y in column (f) and the deferred gain subtracted at column (g).[231]

What is reinvested?

Note that only the gain is reinvested, and not the total proceeds like for a Section 1031 exchange. Any portion of capital gains can be reinvested. The investment must be made with cash, not property. Also, the taxpayer reinvests the funds directly and no Qualified Intermediary is required like for a Section 1031 exchange.

What will be the character of the gain when it's taxable?

When the deferred capital gains become taxable, they keep their character as short-term or long-term at the time of the sale.[232]

Be prepared

The investor should keep a side account of cash or liquid investments to provide for paying the tax on the reinvested gain in 2026.

Since the deferral is accomplished by reducing the tax basis of property held by the Qualified Opportunity Fund, there may be little or no depreciation to offset rental income passed through to the owners.

---

230   Treasury Regulations § 1.1400Z2(a)-1(a)(2).
231   Form 8949 Instructions, page 9.
232   Treasury Regulations § 1.1400Z2(c).

How is the investment done?

The property will usually be acquired by an individual investing in a qualified opportunity fund, and not by a direct investment in the property.

The fund will be organized as a qualified opportunity zone business, conducting a trade or business within a qualified opportunity zone. The assets of the fund, on average, must consist of at least 90% qualified opportunity zone property. There are guidelines in the final regulations to treat property that is being substantially improved over a 30-month period as qualified opportunity zone property.[233]

According to the final regulations, the ownership and operation of real property is a trade or business under the Qualified Opportunity Zone rule, except a triple-net lease is not the active conduct of a trade or business.[234]

An investor with an eligible gain can acquire an equity interest in a Qualified Opportunity Fund (QOF) on or before December 31, 2026 in a secondary market purchase.[235] This can provide liquidity to a QOF investor who realizes a large capital loss to free up capital by selling a QOF interest.

An investor can have a mixed-funds investment in a QOF. Part of the investment can be of deferred gain funds and part of other funds.[236] The gain for the appreciation of the other funds portion will not be tax-free when the property is ultimately sold.

Eligible gain

Only capital gains subject to U.S. income tax are eligible for deferral. Some foreign individuals may be exempt from U.S. tax when selling U.S. property and will be ineligible for deferral.[237] These individuals may elect to waive the treaty exemption.[238]

According the final regulations, the full amount of capital gain, unreduced by any losses, is eligible for deferral.[239]

The 180-day replacement period beginning date

Under the general rule, the 180-day replacement period begins on the day the gain would be recognized for federal income tax purposes if the taxpayer did not make the deferral election.[240]

Under the final Treasury Regulations, the same rule applies for Section 1231 gains taxed

---

233 Treasury Regulations § 1.1400Z2(d)-2(b)(4)(ii).
234 Treasury Regulations § 1.1400Z2(d)-1(d)(iii)(A) and (B).
235 Treasury Regulations § 1.1400Z2(a)-1(c)(5)(iii).
236 Treasury Regulations § 1.1400Z2(a)-1(b)(15).
237 Treasury Regulations § 1.1400Z2(a)-1(b)(11)(ix)(1).
238 Treasury Regulations § 1.1400Z2(a)-1(b)(11)(ix)(2).
239 Treasury Regulations § 1.1400Z2(b)(11)(i)(A)(1).
240 Treasury Regulations § 1.1400Z2(b)(7)(i).

as capital gains as for capital gains – they are unreduced for losses to determine the amount that can be reinvested in a Qualified Opportunity Fund and the 180-day replacement period begins on the sale date. The preamble to the final Treasury Regulations states that the rule that amounts deducted as ordinary Section 1231 losses during the five years preceding the sale must be reclassified to ordinary income for the year of the sale only applies to any Section 1231 gains not reinvested in the Qualified Opportunity Fund for which gain is elected to be deferred.

Under the proposed Treasury Regulations, NET Section 1231 gains (reduced for losses) are eligible for reinvestment and the 180-day replacement period begins on the last day of the taxable year when the gains would otherwise be taxable.[241]

For capital gain dividends received from a RIC (mutual fund) or REIT (real estate investment trust), the general rule is the 180-day period begins on the last day of the shareholder's tax year in which the capital gain dividend would otherwise be recognized.[242] Alternatively, the taxpayer may elect to treat the 180-day period to begin on the date the dividend is received.[243] This usually won't be practical because the taxpayer probably won't know whether the dividend is a capital gain dividend when it is received.

The 180-day period for reinvesting a taxable undistributed capital gain of a RIC or REIT begins the last day of the shareholder's tax year that it would otherwise be recognized. Alternatively, the shareholder may elect for the 180-day period to begin on the last day of the RIC's or REIT's tax year.[244]

For securities sales, the 180-day period begins on the trade date.[245]

The 180-day period for reinvesting a partner's share of an eligible gain begins on the last day of the partnership tax year in which the partner's distributive share of the partnership's eligible gain is taken into account. Alternatively, the partner may elect to begin the 180-day period (1) the same date as the partnership's 180-day period, or (2) the due date for the partnership's federal income tax return, without extensions. (March 15 for a partnership with a calendar year-end.)[246]

There was no election to start the reinvestment period on the due date of the partnership income tax return in the proposed regulations.

Capital gains for payments received after December 31, 2017 for installment sales made before December 22, 2017 are eligible for reinvestment in a Qualified Opportunity Fund.[247]

241	Proposed Treasury Regulations § 1.1400Z2(a)-1(b)(2)(iii).
242	Treasury Regulations § 1.1400Z2(b)(7)(ii)(A).
243	Treasury Regulations § 1.1400Z2(b)(7)(ii)(B).
244	Treasury Regulations § 1.1400Z2(b)(7)(ii)(C)
245	Treasury Regulations § 1.1400Z2(b)(7)(iv)(A).
246	Treasury Regulations § 1.1400Z2(b)(8)(iii).
247	Treasury Regulations § 1.1400Z2(b)(7)(viii)(A).

The 180-day period for gain from installment sales may be treated as the last day of the tax year the capital gain from the payment is taxable or as the date payments are received.[248]

Eligible gains realized by a partnership

If a partnership realizes an eligible capital gain, it can reinvest the gain in a Qualified Opportunity Fund and elect to defer the capital gain. The partnership, not the partners, recognizes the deferred gain at the end of the deferral period, so the partners at that time will report the gain.[249]

If a partnership realizes an eligible capital gain and does not reinvest the gain in a Qualified Opportunity Fund, the individual partners may reinvest their share of the gain in a Qualified Opportunity Fund and elect to defer the capital gain.[250]

Notice that good communication of information to the partners by the management of the partnership is critical for making these elections. I have personally invested in partnerships and had no clue of the amounts of the capital gains until I received Schedule K-1 in August or September for a calendar-year partnership. Electing to reinvest the gain would be impossible in that case.

In addition, partnerships aren't required to distribute the cash from realized capital gains to their partners. The partner might have cash to reinvest a partnership gain in a Qualified Opportunity Fund.

Inclusion events

The sale or liquidation of an interest in a Qualified Opportunity Fund before December 31, 2026 is an inclusion event and the balance of the deferred gain will become taxable at that time.[251] The taxpayer may elect to reinvest that amount into another Qualified Opportunity Fund and the gain. The 180-day reinvestment period starts on the inclusion date and the holding period for ultimate gain inclusion starts all over again on the reinvestment date.[252]

A gift of an interest in a Qualified Opportunity Fund is an inclusion event.[253] So is a transfer between spouses incident to a divorce.[254] (An equal division of a community property interest should not be a transfer because it is already owned by the spouse.)

A transfer of an interest in a Qualified Opportunity Fund as an inheritance after a death is not an inclusion event.[255] The deferred income is income with respect of a

248	Treasury Regulations § 1.1400Z2(b)(7)(viii)(B).	
249	Treasury Regulations § 1.1400Z2(a)-1(c)(7).	
250	Treasury Regulations § 1.1400Z2(a)-1(c)(8).	
251	Treasury Regulations § 1.1400Z2(b)-1(c).	
252	Treasury Regulations § 1.1400Z2(a)-1(b)(11)(iv).	
253	Treasury Regulations § 1.1400Z2(b)-1(c)(3)(i).	
254	Treasury Regulations § 1.1400Z2(b)-1(c)(3)(ii).	
255	Treasury Regulations § 1.1400Z2(b)-1(c)(4).	

decedent, so there is no basis adjustment at death. The beneficiary "steps into the shoes" of the decedent and reports the deferred gain at the earlier of an inclusion event or December 31, 2026.[256] The decedent's holding period is "tacked on" to the holding period of the beneficiary to determine whether the holding period for tax forgiveness of appreciation and up to 15% of the deferred gain applies.[257]

Covid-19 deadline extensions

As a result of a Presidential Order issued on March 13, 2020 declaring the COVID-19 a National Disaster under the Robert T. Stafford Disaster Relief and Emergency Assistance Act, the IRS has announced some relief measured for Qualified Opportunity Funds.[258]

The deadline to reinvest capital gains in a Qualified Opportunity Fund that would have occurred on or after April 1, 2020 and before December 31, 2020 was extended to December 31, 2020.

The COVID-19 pandemic is deemed to be a reasonable cause for a Qualified Opportunity Fund to avoid the penalty for failing to hold at least 90% of its assets as Qualified Opportunity Zone property under Internal Revenue Code Section 1400Z-2(f)(3) when (1) the last day of the first 6-month period of the taxable year or (2) the last day of the taxable year falls within the period beginning on April 1, 2020 and ending on December 31, 2020. No filing for a waiver is required to be excused from the penalty.

A 30-month period for substantial improvement of property held by a Qualified Opportunity Fund or Qualified Opportunity Zone business disregards the period beginning April 1, 2020 and ending on December 31, 2020. (This period, if applicable, is added to the 30-month period.)

A Qualified Opportunity Zone business within a federally declared disaster area may receive up to 24 additional months to expend its working capital assets, as long as the Qualified Opportunity Zone business otherwise meets the requirements of the working capital safe harbor under Treasury Regulations Section 1.14002(d)-1(d)(3)(v).

The 12-month reinvestment period that includes January 20, 2020 is extended up to an additional 12 months to reinvest in Qualified Opportunity Zone property some or all of the proceeds received by the Qualified Opportunity Fund from the return of capital or the sale or disposition of some or all of the Qualified Opportunity Fund's Qualified Opportunity Zone property, provided the Qualified Opportunity Fund satisfies the requirements of Treasury Regulations Section 1.14002(f)-1(b)(a) and invests the proceeds in the manner originally intended before January 20, 2020.

For additional information, see Form 8949, Sale and Other Dispositions of Capital Assets and instructions; Form 8996, Qualified Opportunity Fund and instructions, Form 8997, Initial and Annual Statement of Qualified Opportunity Fund (QOF) Investments and instructions; and Publication 544, Sales and Dispositions of Assets.

---

256   Treasury Regulations § 1.1400Z2(b)-1(c)(4)(iii).
257   Treasury Regulations § 1.1400Z2(b)-1(d)(1)(iii).
258   Notice 2020-23 and Notice 2020-39.